THE SAFEBOOK

81 Super-Important Things You Should Know about Your Safety

Seema Chari is an author, quizmaster, anchor and media professional. She has written more than 20 books on general knowledge, quizzing and trivia, and fiction for young readers.

As co-founder of Xpress Minds Edutainment, India's leading quizzing company, she has conducted nationwide quizzes, including the INTACH Heritage Quiz, Nobel Quiz, *Bharat ko Jaaniye* Global Quiz, as well as the National Safety Science Quiz for over 75,000 school children, while setting up Safety Clubs in multiple schools across India.

Seema obtained her BA in English Literature from Women's Christian College, Chennai, and followed up with an MA from JNU, an M. Phil from Delhi University and a Masters in Didactics from the University of Venice.

She speaks seven languages, writes and directs plays, has acted on stage and screen, and sung for A.R. Rahman. She loves travelling by road, drinking filter coffee, dabbling in trivia, and solving crosswords, sudoku and jigsaw puzzles.

THE SAFEBOOK

81 Super-Important Things You Should Know about Your Safety

SEEMA CHARI

Illustrations by Mistunee Chowdhury

hachette INDIA

First published in 2022 by Hachette India
(Registered name: Hachette Book Publishing India Pvt. Ltd)
An Hachette UK company
www.hachetteindia.com

1

ISBN: 978-93-91028-96-1

Hachette Book Publishing India Pvt. Ltd
4th & 5th Floors, Corporate Centre
Plot No. 94, Sector 44, Gurugram – 122003, India

Typeset by Manmohan Kumar, Delhi

Printed and bound in India
by Manipal Technologies Limited

FSC www.fsc.org MIX Paper from responsible sources FSC™ C043100

CONTENTS

Four: ON THE ROAD

Five: FOOD

Six: THE INTERNET

AUTHOR SAYS HI – AND WHY!

Dear Reader,

Thank you for picking up *The SafeBook*.

We live in a country (and world) where children are increasingly exposed to unsafe situations – our roads are more chaotic, we live surrounded by devices and cables, cybercrime is getting more frequent and more incisive, targeting younger and younger people, chemicals lurk in personal and food products, while climate change and human apathy are leading to more 'natural' disasters than ever before.

Since forearmed is forewarned, I do urge you to leaf through this book – open it anywhere, on any chapter – read, understand and be informed. Each chapter presents situations that can occur in our daily lives, some dos and don'ts, the science behind the main phenomena or actions, and points to focus on if things go awry. There are short quizzes scattered across the book, some trivia, some suggestions and some activities.

You might say (or think) the Internet is stuffed to the brim with answers, so why buy a *book*?

Here are has some distinct advantages I believe *The SafeBook* has over the Internet:

1. The information in this book can be read, understood and followed by young readers.
2. The descriptions and instructions have been compiled from international as well as India-specific sources.
3. Information is provided to the point, without excessive and often overly technical terminology.
4. As far as possible, all situations presented are relevant to children across India, and the safety actions can be carried out by them (note: we recommend adult supervision *wherever and whenever* possible, which is *everywhere*).
5. The SafeBook is made of paper, so even if you drop it by mistake, it won't break :)!

While the book can be read and mostly understood by even 10-year-old readers, a word of caution: safety is serious business, and lack of safety can quickly turn to grave danger. So dear parents, please read this book with your kids; being safety smart is age-agnostic.

I gratefully acknowledge the research put in by Drona Vatsyayan, a friend and young physicist now doing his doctorate in Spain, in ensuring that the descriptions and advice in the book are backed by solid science.

Happy reading and stay safe!

~ Seema Chari

Please note: The SafeBook *has been compiled for laypersons by a layperson. Every attempt has been made to present scientifically and factually sound information. However, all actions and advice are indicative and neither binding nor statutory.*

Section One

FIRE

1 WHAT CAUSES A FIRE?

Fire is perhaps the most important discovery of human civilization. It helps us cook our food, keeps people warm in the cold, and, hey, lights up birthday candles. But it can also destroy entire forests, burn down buildings and injure people. What exactly is a fire made of?

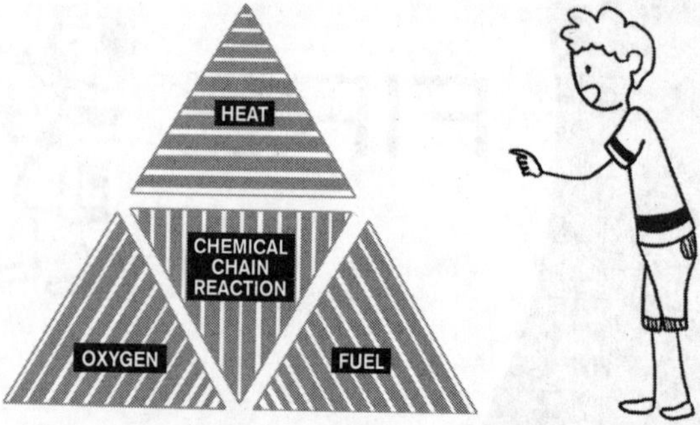

Fire tetrahedron or triangle

Scientists call fire 'combustion', meaning 'burning'. It is a chemical reaction* (*see next page*) that produces heat and light. Combustion needs four factors to be present. Together, they form the Fire

Tetrahedron (a figure with four sides or faces): oxygen, heat, fuel and a chemical reaction. All four factors need to be present, otherwise there will be no combustion.

- A **fuel** is a material that can easily catch fire and burn.
- When the fuel burns, it reacts with **oxygen** in the air – producing heat and light.
- A **heat** source starts a fire or 'ignites' the fuel at the beginning. It allows a fire to spread by heating any fuels nearby.
- The **chain reaction** allows the fire to spread and continue until and unless at least one of the elements of the fire tetrahedron is blocked.

SafeBook Says

> **Putting out a fire, or fire extinction, works on the blocking of any of the three main elements of the fire tetrahedron. A fire can be *cooled* (by removing heat), *starved* (by removing fuel) or *smothered* (by removing oxygen). Fire extinguishers work on the basic principle of removing oxygen and heat.**

**Chemical Reaction: two or more things, called reactants, come together, and form a third thing, such that you can never get the original two things again. Think of these examples: add lime juice and milk and you'll get cottage cheese or paneer. Crack an egg over a hot pan and you'll get a fried egg. You will never get the milk or raw egg back. In the same way, if a thing burns, it will never come back.*

2 HOW THE CHIMNEY EFFECT CAN MAKE A FIRE WORSE

Has a chimney ever caught your attention? It's not just a vent for smoke from a fire, from which highly toxic substances, like carbon monoxide, go out into the atmosphere. Buildings also sometimes enable or allow for air to flow upwards, an event called the 'chimney' or 'stack' effect, which can turn around and aggravate a fire.

Quick Science

Firstly, this happens when a fire breaks out and releases hot air. Since hot air rises upwards, it creates a pressure difference between the inside and outside of a building due to the difference in temperatures, and draws cooler air from below (the base).

The trapped hot air can find its way out even through small openings and window frames. Meanwhile, air from the outside comes in to make up for the escaped air.

In many homes in the West, and colder parts of India, this air feeds the fireplace just below the chimney, thus the name 'Chimney Effect', but it is also called the Stack Effect.

In summer, the reverse of this effect happens. The warm air that enters the building into the upper floors mixes, due to the pressure difference, with the cool air already there within the building and then sinks to the lowermost parts of the building.

If there is fire, smoke can rush in via stairwells and air-conditioning ducts due to this 'reverse' chimney effect and make it even more difficult to escape the fire. This can be especially deadly in high-rise buildings.

SafeBook Says

"If you are trapped in a fire, you should cover all openings, and if possible, close the doors as you escape to restrict this chimney-effect air flow."

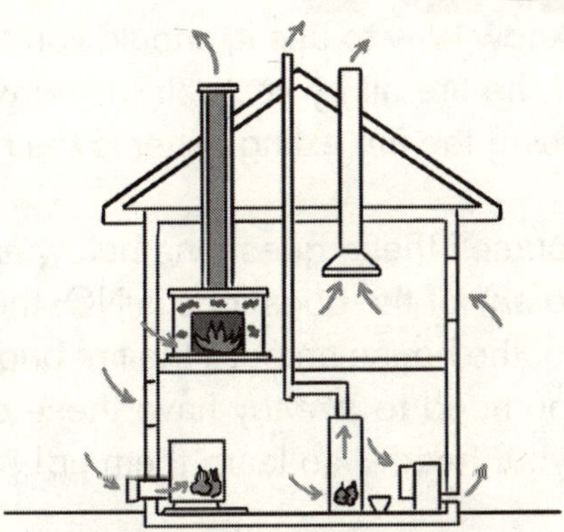

The Chimney Effect

3 WHEN TO CALL THE FIRE BRIGADE

What if a fire breaks out somewhere in your house? What should you do first? Try to douse the fire? Run out of the place? Or find your phone in the scramble and call 101?

You might look for a bucket of water and try to extinguish the fire yourself – but remember, you must be very careful about using water on certain fires.

Let's say that you also have a fire extinguisher and you know how to use it, should you then try to get rid of the fire all by yourself? How would you know if using the fire extinguisher is the right thing to do?

Ask yourself these questions below and if your answer to *any* of the questions is NO, then *please* step out of the house and call the fire brigade. This means you need to *already* have these questions ready in your head – so learn them up!

Quick Checklist

Run these questions in your head if you ever encounter a fire.

- ☐ Do you have the right type of fire extinguisher to match the type of fire?
- ☐ Is the fire extinguisher large enough to put out the fire?
- ☐ Is the fire small and contained (like in a bin, pan, etc.)?
- ☐ Is there a safe way to exit the area quickly if your attempts to extinguish the flames are unsuccessful?
- ☐ Is the area free of other fire hazards such as newspapers, drapery, gas cylinders, and so on?

If the answer to any of these is NO, quickly EXIT.

Remember!

If you smell gas at home, open the windows and doors, switch off the gas main and step out. If you use an LPG cylinder, do not touch the cylinder. Contact the gas company.

SafeBook Says

"The fire brigade number in India is 101 and you should call the number immediately in case of a fire. It is important that you provide all details on the call such as:
a. Your address,
b. Your contact number, and
c. A description of the fire."

The fire department should be called immediately as anything, even the smallest spark, might cause the gas to ignite and explode.

4 HOW TO USE A FIRE EXTINGUISHER

You've seen a fire extinguisher, right? That red-coloured cylinder fitted against the wall in public places? You must have come across them at schools, malls, cinema halls and (hopefully) at home as well. You might have also seen how it works on TV or on the Internet. But have you ever given a thought to how to use it if, heaven forbid, you need to put out a fire?

We're guessing you haven't. In fact, a lot of people don't how to use a fire extinguisher even if they have it in place.

So here's the science first. Fire extinguishers put out a fire by taking away one or more elements of the fire triangle/tetrahedron. Fire safety, at its most basic, is based upon the principle of keeping fuel sources and ignition sources separate.

First of all, you must learn what type of extinguisher is to be – or *not* to be – used on what type of fires. Here's a quick table to help you know about extinguishing agents and fire sources.

Symbols on fire extinguishers and what they mean. These may vary.

	RED Water	LIGHT YELLOW Foam spray	BLUE ABC powder	BLACK Carbon dioxide	BRIGHT YELLOW Wet chemical
A Wood, paper, textiles	✓	✓	✓	✗	✓
B Flammable liquids	✗	✓	✓	✓	✗
C Flammable gases	✗	✗	✓	✗	✗
Electrical Equipment	✗	✗	✓	✓	✗
F Cooking Oils and Fats	✗	✗	✗	✗	✓

Once you know what to use, remember the acronym PASS:

1. **P**ull the pin.
2. **A**im the nozzle at the base of the fire.
3. **S**queeze the trigger.
4. **S**weep the nozzle from side to side until the fire is put out.

Quick Tips

- Fire extinguishers can only take out fires at initial stages. If a fire is taller than you, then your extinguisher will be no match for it. Call the fire brigade immediately!
- A gauge meter on the extinguisher helps you check if it is fully charged and pressurized. If it is on the lower side, it won't put out the fire.

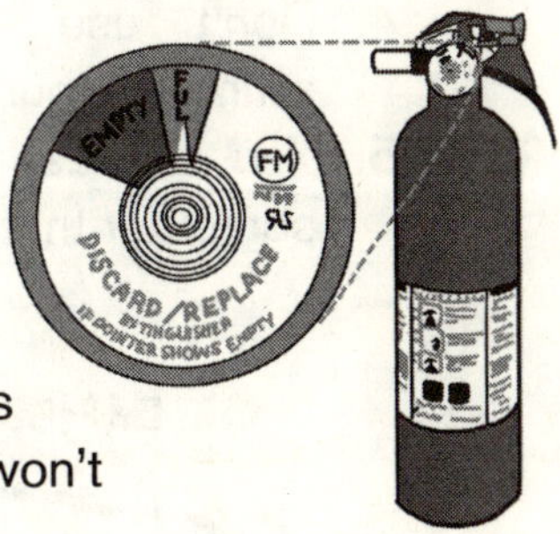

- Your safety is your first priority, so if the room is filled with smoke, head out!
- Even if the fire appears extinguished, do not turn your back on it. Look for hot spots or hidden fires that might reignite at any moment.
- Install models that are handy and easy to use and ensure they are certified by testing authorities. Be alert – and ask the grown-ups to make sure of this!

SafeBook Quiz

True or False? Write T or F.

1. You can put out burning oil by using water.
2. Foam should not be used for extinguishing home fires.
3. An electric fire of up to 1000 volts can be put out by dry powder.
4. Don't use carbon dioxide to extinguish burning wood.
5. You can use wet chemical on a computer that catches fire.

SafeBook Says

"The most used extinguishers are the ABC type. They are meant to cover almost all kinds of household fires and are generally recommended. They use a dry chemical extinguisher, which is a fine dry powder to coat the fire's fuel and cut off its oxygen supply."

5 WHAT TO DO IF THERE'S A FIRE IN THE KITCHEN

Where in a house are fire accidents most likely to happen? Did you say 'kitchen'? Yup, guessed right. And when there is a fire in the kitchen, you need to act fast before things get out of control.

Quick Action

A. Fire in a cooking pan:

1. Cover it with a lid.
2. Take it off the burner.
3. Turn off the stove.

B. Fire in the oven:

1. Make sure that the oven door is closed.
2. Switch off the power supply.

DO

☑ Keep a small fire extinguisher in the kitchen.

DON'T

☒ Use water on grease/oil fires as water and oil don't mix and it will further spread the fire. Instead use large amounts of baking soda on the fire.

☒ Leave any cooking item unattended.

☒ Wear loose clothing while cooking – and please roll up long sleeves.

☒ Use metal containers in the microwave.

☒ Ignore spills, and make sure there is no grease build-up.

☒ Keep flammable items like paper rolls, cleaning rags and food packaging near the stove

SafeBook Quiz

Which of these would you use to put out a grease fire? Tick the right answer.

☐ Flour

☐ Baking soda

6 IF YOUR CLOTHES CATCH FIRE...

It's a nightmare come true when clothes accidentally brush against a flame or a spark, and catch fire. Ever wondered what one should do then?

What should you definitely not do?

The one thing that you should definitely *not do* is run. Clothes on fire cause serious burns to the wearer and can also lead to permanent injuries, and worse.

Quick Action

There is little or no time to lose. Remember this simple mantra by heart and repeat it daily:

STOP,

DROP

and ROLL.

Stop *where you are.*

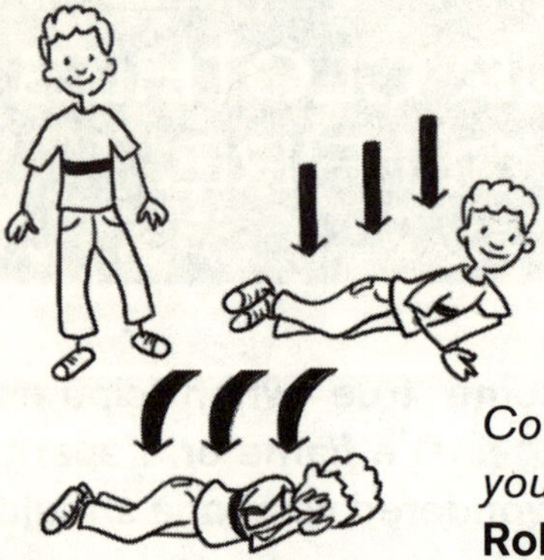

Drop *to the floor.*

Cover your face with your hands and…
Roll *until the flames are extinguished.*

Finally, cool a burn with running water (*not* ice, because ice can stick to your clothes and aggravate the wound).

DO

When you're in the kitchen (or by a campfire, or the chemistry lab's Bunsen burner, or even near a candle or lantern...

☑ Always choose clothes with 'low fire-danger' labelling.

☑ Choose close-fitting rather than loose clothes that can swing away from the body and catch fire.

☑ Remember that fabrics such as silk and wool are difficult to ignite and burn slowly when they catch fire.

☑ Remember that synthetic fibres are hard to ignite but once alight, melt and cause severe burns. Polyester, chiffon, rayon, nylon, georgette, taffeta and similar lightweight fabrics are all synthetic.

SafeBook Says

"Heavy, tight-weave fabrics will burn more slowly than light, loose-weave fabrics of the same material."

7 HOW TO PREPARE A FIRE-ESCAPE PLAN

Unforeseen events like house fires are more common than you imagine, and they end up causing a lot of damage. If and when such events occur, the first thing that happens (and spreads) is PANIC, which can affect your ability to think rationally, and that means precious time is wasted. The first few seconds are extremely valuable for the safety and well-being of you and your family.

You can be a step ahead if you have a well-thought-out plan prepared for situations like these. Also, do a mock drill at least twice a year (it could even be fun to do one!).

Quick Action

- Take a tour of your house with your family and note all the exit points (read: doors and windows). If you live on a higher floor, windows are NOT a great exit point.

- Try and find at least *two* ways out of each room and check if all escape routes are easily accessible (for example, it is NOT a good idea to place heavy furniture or plants near or at an exit point.)
- Agree on a safe spot to serve as your meeting place afterwards. Look for landmarks so that it is easier to remember.
- Consider the age and special needs of members who might find it difficult to escape on their own. For the same reason, assign an elder and a back-up person to a younger person to help them escape.
- Install at least one ABC type fire extinguisher per level and smoke detectors near the places where fire is most likely to break out.
- Take a blueprint of the house plan and mark the route and exits. Share it with all members and overnight guests. Put it up throughout the

SafeBook Says

"A small flame can go completely out of control and turn into a major fire in less than 30 seconds. It takes only 1 minute for thick black smoke to fill up a house."

house (like behind the door in each room) to make it accessible for everyone. Draw it here!

MY HOUSE PLAN

8 IF YOU SEE FIRE OUTSIDE YOUR ROOM...

A fire could be caused by things not in your control. However, what you can do is be prepared if a fire ever breaks out in your house.

The first step is to have an escape plan that every family member should be aware of.

Remember!

You only have THREE MINUTES to get out safely.

Smoke from fire can make it hard to figure out the exit path, therefore it is important that you conduct fire drills at home regularly, at least twice a year. The flowchart outlined on the next page will come to your rescue as you escape fire.

SafeBook Says

> **"If, for some reason, you cannot get out, make sure that you block the gaps under the door with towels, clothes or blankets (preferably wet) to keep the heat and smoke out. Also cover your mouth with a wet cloth to avoid breathing in the smoke."**

Quick Action

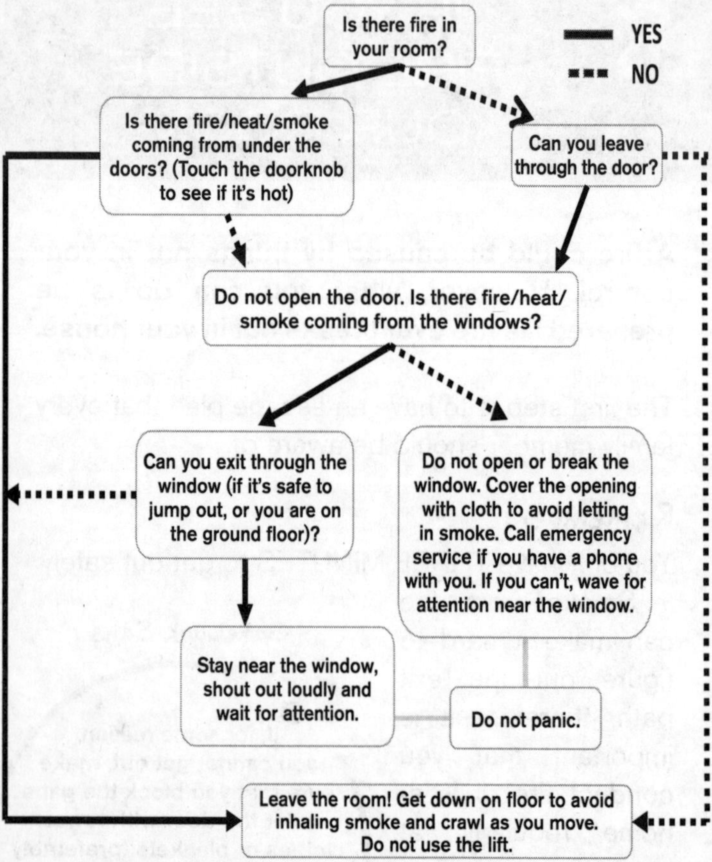

9 HOW TO ESCAPE A FIRE

What if a fire were to break out where you are? Fires are scary. A couple of seconds here and there and the situation could become life-threatening. The panic will be much less if you are aware of what you need to do. That's where an escape plan comes in handy, but even if there's none, it is important to remember the way out.

Here are the steps you need to follow, but always remember that the key is to stay low to the ground as you escape. SMOKE OFTEN HURTS MORE PEOPLE THAN FLAMES DO, BECAUSE SMOKE MEANS LESS OXYGEN. Since smoke rises upwards, staying close to the ground makes it easier to breathe and to see better through the haze.

DO

- ☑ Identify the exits and get out immediately if you see flames or smoke.
- ☑ Close the doors while leaving to stop the fire from spreading.

- ☑ Check if the doorknob is warm before opening any door. If it is warm, it's likely that there's a fire on the other side; look for a different exit.
- ☑ Always use the staircase to exit.
- ☑ Remember to **S**top, **D**rop and **R**oll if your clothes are likely to catch fire.
- ☑ Once you are out, call the fire brigade.

DON'T

- ☒ Go looking for valuables – life is priceless!
- ☒ Use lifts. They might break or stop, and you will be trapped inside.

If you can't get out

DO

- ☑ Place wet towels or blankets under the door to keep the smoke out.
- ☑ See if you can escape out a window.
- ☑ Else, yell for help and keep your mouth covered with a towel to keep yourself from directly breathing in smoke.

DON'T

- ☒ Hide under a bed or inside a closet; this makes it difficult for a firefighter to locate you.

SafeBook Says

> **"50 to 80 per cent of fire-related deaths are caused by smoke inhalation, making it the largest cause of fire-related injuries."**

10 WHAT CATCHES FIRE EASILY?

You would have seen a flammable mark on deodorant bottles.

But what does 'flammable' even mean? Confusingly, flammable and inflammable mean the same thing – something that is capable of burning! Things that can burn but less vigorously, or take a little longer to ignite (catch fire), are called combustible.

Our homes and other common spaces have many liquids lurking around that are flammable that we aren't aware of. Although they do not pose a direct threat, it is important to keep them away from flame sources such as candles and stoves.

Common Flammables

- *Nail Polish Remover*: One of the most common flammable household liquids, the vapours produced by it are flammable and can ignite with any nearby flames.

- *Aerosol Cans*: A lot of household products these days are contained in aerosol cans. including party foams. You should always spray them away from any open flame and keep them away from heat appliances as well.
- *Hand Sanitizers*: Since they contain alcohol, they are capable of causing second- and third-degree burns if they come in contact with a flame. This is super-important to know, especially now in our post-COVID world.
- *Flour*: Due to its large surface area, flour allows flames to travel faster and should be kept away from the stove top. It should never be used to extinguish a fire. It will only worsen the situation.

SafeBook Says

"In this post-COVID age, hand sanitizers are found in every home and in many public places. Read the labels carefully and if you have access to a washbasin and soap, wash your hands with soap and water."

Common things that can catch fire easily

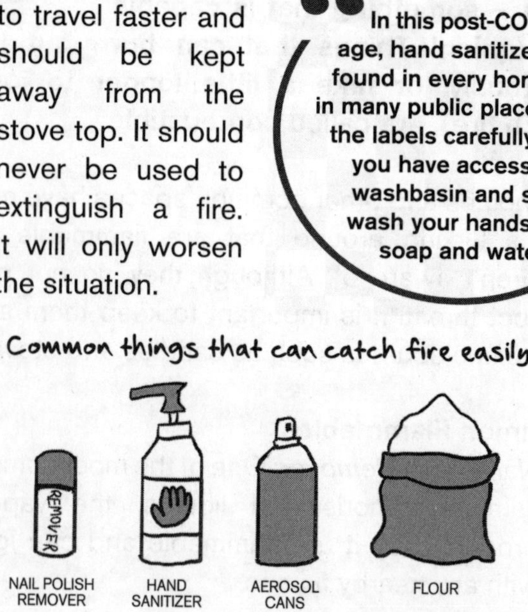

11 WHY WATER IS A NO-NO FOR SOME FIRES

When you think of putting out a fire, what is the first thing that comes to mind?

Water, right? Hmm...

Water is certainly the most used fire extinguisher, but sometimes, it can do more harm than good.

Water or water-based extinguishers should *only* be used on fires starting from organic materials (derived from living matter, such as plants). Fires that involve organic materials are called Class A fires and make up the majority of fires overall.

Tick the organic materials in this set:

☐ WOOD
☐ PAPER
☐ PLASTIC
☐ COTTON
☐ OIL
☐ ELECTRIC WIRE

SafeBook Says

> **"Water is the only agent which has the unique ability to block all three sides of the fire triangle and is also the only suppressant that does not negatively impact the environment."**

For other kinds of fires:

DO

☑ Keep a carbon dioxide (CO_2) or dry-chemical based extinguisher alongside your water fire-extinguisher to fight electric fires or fires caused by flammable liquids such as oil and petrol.

DON'T

☒ Spray water on electrical fires. Water conducts electricity and will cause the fire to spread. Plus, you could get an electric shock.

☒ Spray water on fires caused by flammable liquids such as oil and petrol. These liquids do not mix with water. Instead, water helps in spreading the fire much faster, and this will actually cause greater damage.

☒ Spray water on metal fires involving sodium, magnesium, lithium, titanium, zirconium and others. Such metals could be used in tech products, jewellery and other industries. They are likely to be in the form of sawdust or shavings, which means tiny bits spread over a greater surface area, which increases the possibility of catching fire. In these cases, if water is added, the metal is immediately stripped of its oxygen atom, leaving hydrogen behind. Hydrogen is highly explosive in nature.

12 FIRES DURING FESTIVALS

We all love a good festival, don't we? Many festivals actually include fire as a symbolic element, for purity or sacredness, like before Holi or on Lohri, or the use of firecrackers, even though they are banned in many states. Here's how to be cautious and careful during festivities.

DON'T

- ☒ Place *diyas* or candles near items that can burn or melt easily. Keep them away from curtains and furniture!
- ☒ Light firecrackers, even if it is Diwali. But if you *must* get crackers, buy 'green crackers' from

a licensed manufacturer, if permitted in your state/area.

☒ Wear long and loose clothing – it can fly, sway and swish, and brush against flames and set *you* alight. Synthetic clothes can melt and cause severe burns.

☒ Hang around a smoky fire for very long. Smoke from a bonfire is super-harmful for both the eyes and lungs, and can cause discomfort and irritation in both.

☒ Leave a bonfire unattended. It could turn into a huge fire hazard. Make sure a bonfire either goes out or is completely extinguished before leaving the site. It must be damped with water to ensure that no sparks are left.

DO

☑ Be careful with what is thrown into the bonfire. Even for fun, do *not* throw aerosol cans, batteries or any flammable liquid. They will explode and lead to an uncontrolled blaze.

☑ Use only dry wood for a bonfire.

SafeBook Says

"Before lighting up a bonfire, check it. Small children and animals could have hidden inside the pile, out of curiosity or for fun – they need to be cajoled out! And no, that's not a joke."

13 TAKING CARE AROUND CANDLES

Be it a birthday, Diwali or Christmas, candles have a special beauty about them. On top of that, scented candles smell so good. They also come to your rescue when there's a power cut and you don't have a backup supply.

Candles of different kinds have also become popular in households for non-emergency use and for displays in public areas at weddings, pujas and other celebrations. Pretty as it may look, a candle is an open flame and thus a potential fire hazard, and like a stove flame, you should never leave one unattended. And, yes, don't use inflammable candleholders either.

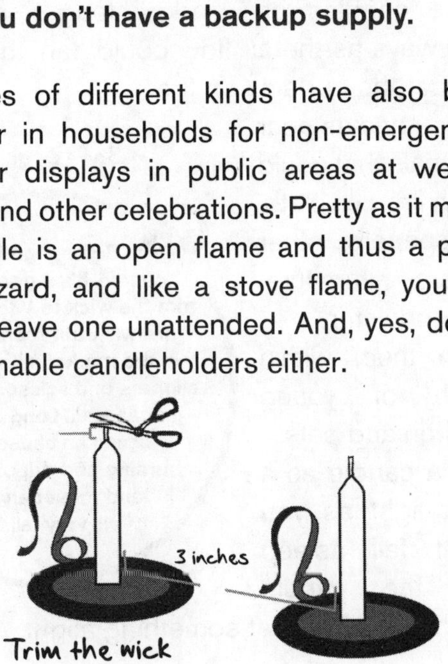

DO

- ☑ Ensure that nothing is placed within one foot of any burning candle. There should be a distance of at least three inches between two candles wherever you are lighting them.
- ☑ Place candles on dry and sturdy surfaces, never on wobbly ones.
- ☑ Keep burning candles within sight at all times.

Remember: When you go out, blow it out!

DON'T

- ☒ Place candles on window ledges or near entryways as the air flow could 'fan' the flame and set the curtains on fire.
- ☒ Place candles near materials that could catch fire, i.e., cloth, newspapers, other papers, furniture, and upholstery.
- ☒ Keep them within reach of young children and pets.
- ☒ Use a candle as a night light as you might fall asleep and the candle could tip over or set something alight.

SafeBook Says

"Before lighting a candle, it's a good idea to trim the wick to ¼th inch. There are wick-trimmers available in the market, although nail-clippers and scissors do the job just as well. Long or crooked wicks can cause uneven burning and dripping of wax, and most dangerous of all, very tall flames."

14 WHAT SHOULD YOU DO IF YOU SMELL GAS?

Have you ever smelled a strong odour of rotten eggs coming from your kitchen? Chances are you have just detected a gas leak. It could be that someone has forgotten to turn the stove knob completely off or there could be some fault in the pipes or fittings.

Natural gas is not dangerous when it is sealed tight inside pipes and is thus widely used as an energy source. But when it leaks, it becomes dangerous – it is highly flammable and can spread quickly. Unchecked gas leaks can increase the risk of fire and explosion. However, the rotten-egg-like smell helps to identify the leak and one can quickly take the proper steps to prevent a potential fire hazard.

DO

- ☑ Open all the doors and windows to let in fresh air.
- ☑ Turn off the gas knob, the gas supply knob or the regulator on the cylinder to completely cut off the gas supply.

- ☑ Turn off electric switches to prevent the gas from interacting with an electric spark.
- ☑ If the smell is too strong and is everywhere in the house, vacate the house immediately and call emergency services.

DON'T

- ☒ Use any other naked flame, i.e., matchsticks, candles or lighters anywhere in the house until the house is completely gas-free. This could take several hours.
- ☒ Use your phones – they could also create a spark.
- ☒ Wait to open doors and windows.

SafeBook Says

> **Liquid Petroleum Gas or LPG is the fuel used for cooking, which comes as piped gas or in cylinders. It is basically made up of propane and butane, and is odourless in its natural state. The smell that you notice when there is a leak is that of ethyl mercaptan, which is added to the LPG precisely to help detect a leak.**

15 HOW TO DEAL WITH AN ELECTRICAL FIRE

With so many electrical appliances in daily use, the chances of a fire breaking out because of them are, sadly, quite high, and most electrical fires these days are caused by faulty or overloaded appliances. Here's how to be prepared…

Electrical fires are usually much more destructive because of the presence of continuous wiring throughout the house and the origin-points of the fires are also difficult to locate when the wiring is within the walls.

SafeBook Says

"**According to the National Crime Record Bureau, more than 7 per cent of all fires are caused by electrical short circuits. Electrical fires can be prevented by using certified appliances and by avoiding the overloading of outlets.**"

Remember!

If you notice an electrical fire, you should call the fire brigade immediately.

Meanwhile, it will help to know more about what to do if you notice an electrical fire:

First find the device that caused the fire. Here are some ifs and thens. Match them!

IF	THEN
1. You can reach the outlet (plug) safely…	A. Ask a grown-up to try using baking soda to extinguish it. The appliance can also be covered with a fire blanket to cut off the oxygen supply. 
2. You are unable to unplug the appliance…	B. Get out immediately, evacuate the building and call the fire department. **101**
3. The fire is small…	C. You can use water to douse the fire in the nearby areas or areas that can be reignited. 
4. You are unable to extinguish the fire…	D. Switch off the main power supply. 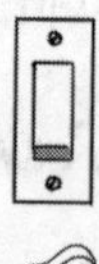
5. When you are absolutely sure the electricity is cut off…	E. Unplug it. 

Section Two

HOME

16 WHAT SHOULD YOU KEEP IN YOUR FIRST-AID BOX?

A first-aid kit is an essential item for all homes. Kits come in all shapes and sizes ranging from basic to comprehensive, and can be found online as well as in stores. However, making a first-aid kit for yourself is an easy and exciting activity. Go do it now!

A home first-aid kit should contain items to treat minor injuries and wounds as well as medicines to treat infections, fever and allergies. To start making one, choose a container that is lightweight, easy to carry and simple to open. Inexpensive nylon bags, waist pouches or make-up cases can also be used. Check your kit twice a year for expired products.

Quick List

Tick the items to make sure you've got everything.

- ☐ First-aid manual and emergency phone numbers
- ☐ Sterile gauze pads
- ☐ Adhesive tapes, bandages (Band-Aids)
- ☐ Crêpe bandage

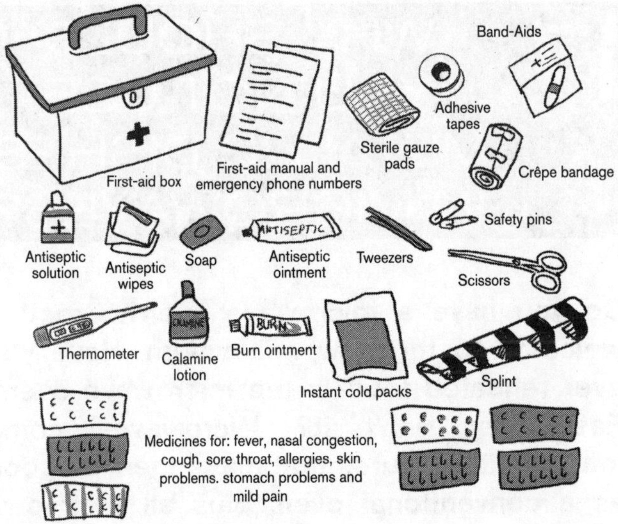

- ☐ Antiseptic solution, wipes, soap and ointment
- ☐ Antibiotic ointment
- ☐ Tweezers, scissors, and safety pins
- ☐ Thermometer
- ☐ Calamine lotion
- ☐ Burn ointment
- ☐ Instant cold packs
- ☐ Alcohol wipes
- ☐ Splint
- ☐ Medicines

SafeBook Says

> **"According to the International Standardization Organization (ISO), all first-aid kits should be marked with a GREEN-COLOURED PLUS SIGN. Pick up that green sketch pen right away!"**

17 WHY SHOULD YOU NOT USE METALLIC DISHES IN MICROWAVES?

Do you have a microwave oven? Great! – welcome to the new millennium. Have you ever reheated food in the microwave oven? Easy-peasy, isn't it? Microwaves come loaded with features that make them as good as a conventional oven, plus all their own conveniences. But there's more to it.

Now here's the biggie: by any chance, have you used a plate, fork, spoon, knife, or even aluminium foil in a microwave? *Spark! Bang! Phttack!* Whoa, hold your horses right there, and read on!

Q: How does a microwave oven work?

A: On the principle of ELECTROMAGNETIC RADIATION.

Did we hear you say, 'Huh'?

A transmitter inside emits (what else!) microwaves that jiggle the water molecules inside your food. As these molecules start moving around, their movement creates heat, the water turns into steam and your food gets hot. Pretty nifty trick, right?

Now, there are two problems with metals:

1. They are dense solids and as their own molecules heat up, they can't move around like water. Instead, they vibrate, and the metal heats up quickly. You do remember that metals are good conductors of heat? Eventually, THEY CAN CATCH FIRE. Oops!
2. Metals can reflect microwaves instead of absorbing them (try catching your own reflection in a stainless-steel dish. It's like a strange mirror). So the microwaves start bouncing from one surface to the other. Eventually, (oh dear, this is like déjà vu!), THEY CAN CATCH FIRE.

So, what is safe to use in microwave ovens? Containers made of glass, ceramic, fibre, but without any metallic design features – not even metallic paint.

DO

- ☑ Remember to keep the vents (the holes or slits in the microwave oven) clear.
- ☑ Always follow the manufacturer's instructions. If in doubt, double-check with them. Instructions and manuals for many brands are available on the Internet.

- ☑ Make sure your microwave is properly cleaned and there is no build-up of grease or dirt.
- ☑ Use dishes that clearly state that they are microwave safe. The icons for microwave safe look like these:

DON'T

- ☒ Store objects on top of your microwave oven, or any other appliances. They can block ventilation and cause extra heat to build up in the appliance.
- ☒ Use metal containers in the microwave. What happens when you do?

  The microwaves cannot penetrate the metal, but they will cause an electric current

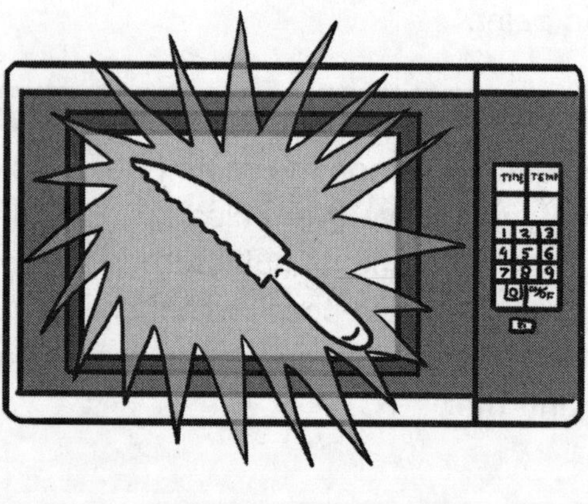

in the utensil. If the metal has jagged edges, then 'arcing' can make sparks fly. It can be quite scary, and with good reason – If there is something combustible in the oven, it can cause a fire.

☒ Power microwaves using extension leads.

☒ Ignore spills.

☒ **Simplest rule:** DON'T USE A DAMAGED MICROWAVE. Get it repaired immediately.

SafeBook Says

"Arcing can also happen if the inside of the microwave is damaged and the microwaves reflect off the inner walls, which are chrome-plated and thus reflective. Interestingly, dirty sponges, wetted and placed in a microwave oven and heated at 1000 watt power for a few minutes can lose a significant amount of bacteria such as *E. coli*, coliforms and MS2 phages. So not just your food, your cleaning things can also get safer to use!"

18 HOW TO HANDLE A STEAM IRON

Do you iron your own clothes? No, let's change the question a little. Do you know *how* to iron clothes? Without getting scorch marks on your clothes or blisters on your fingers and arm? Bravo!

The basic steps of using a steam iron look easy:

1. Pour a little water into the marked cavity of the iron, and switch it on.
2. Place your cloth on an ironing board or on a flat and hard surface.

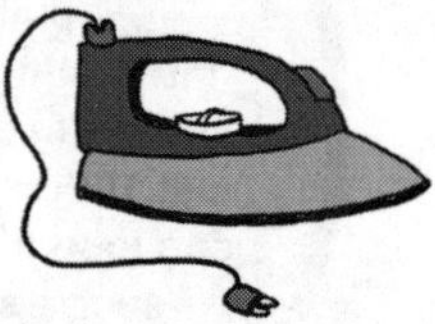

3. Wait for the indicator light to go off, which means the iron is heated up sufficiently and is ready for use.
4. Press the nozzle to spray some water on the cloth, and start moving the hot iron on the cloth.

But, of course, IT'S NOT THAT EASY. There's one more thing that you need to take care of.

Fabrics vary and each fabric needs a different amount of heat. Linen and cotton can withstand high heat, while silk and wool need mild heat. Nylon needs the least amount of heat, so you will need to use the lowest heat setting. If you apply too much heat on a fabric that cannot bear it, the cloth will get scorched or, worse, stick to the iron and never come off.

How do you figure out just how much heat to apply on a garment? *Easy*: just check the tags to identify the fabric. Sometimes clothes even have the iron's heat setting marked on the tag. And if you have had the garment stitched by a tailor and are not sure, start with the lowest heat and slowly increase the heat if you feel the item is just not getting pressed properly.

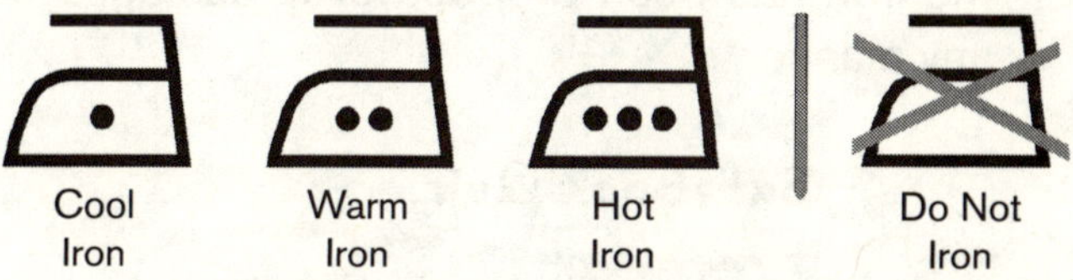

Heat setting symbols for irons

DO

☑ Use an iron only for its intended use – that is, on clothes and fabrics. Do NOT use it, for instance, to iron hair. That's dumb and super-dangerous!

☑ Always disconnect the iron from the outlet before filling with water, emptying, or when not in use.

- ☑ Always turn off the iron before plugging or unplugging from the power outlet.
- ☑ Let the iron cool completely before putting away, and always keep it out of reach of small children and pets.
- ☑ Loop the cord loosely around the iron when storing it.

DON'T

- ☒ Yank out the cord; instead, hold the plug firmly and pull to disconnect.
- ☒ Allow the cord to touch hot surfaces.
- ☒ Immerse the iron in water or other liquids.
- ☒ Operate the iron with a damaged cord, or if the iron has been dropped or is damaged in any manner.

SafeBook Quiz

What setting should be used for woollen clothes?

- ☐ Low
- ☐ Warm
- ☐ Hot

19 KEEPING FOOD SAFE IN THE REFRIGERATOR

Picture this scenario. A nice hot meal is cooked. But you aren't hungry. So you bung the dish into the fridge until later. Makes sense, right? No, not really. It will make the fridge work harder (read: drink up much more power and finally add to your electricity bill).

At the same time, food must be refrigerated within two hours of cooking, else bacteria can start multiplying. Here are a few more hints.

Quick Tips

- If you are planning to freeze food, use only specially designed freezer bags or plastic containers without empty spaces that can trap air, as that's what causes frozen foods to deteriorate.

- Perishable foods should be refrigerated at no more than 4°C within two hours of preparation. For an Indian summer, make that one hour or less!
- Dividing food into smaller portions makes cooling faster.
- Cover liquids when you refrigerate them. If left uncovered, they can release moisture and make the poor compressor work harder.

SafeBook Says

> **If you let food sit out for more than two hours, you cannot make it safe by reheating. Toxins produced by certain bacteria such as *Staphylococcus* (staph) and *Bacillus cereus* cannot be destroyed by high cooking temperatures.**

20 INVISIBLE DANGEROUS CHEMICALS LURKING AT HOME

Let us zoom in on some chemicals that are present in common daily-use items, ranging from shampoos to skin creams. Direct and prolonged exposure to such chemicals can lead to respiratory problems, interfere with body growth and is said to increase the risk of diseases such as cancer.

Quick List

Read the labels closely for...

- **Phthalates:** These are used as softening agents in plastics and skincare products. They affect the endocrine system of the body, and can lead to liver and kidney problems, asthma and cancer. The endocrine system is made up of glands that produce and release the hormones that control nearly all the processes in your body, such as coordinating how the body functions, metabolism, growth and development, and emotions and sleep.

- **Parabens:** These are preservatives used in shampoos, toothpastes and cosmetics. Like phthalates, they also affect the endocrine system. This is why many baby products proudly proclaim 'paraben-free' on their labels.
- **Lead:** Found in paints and some make-up products, lead is a toxic metal that can affect the nervous system of the body, causing brain damage and other issues. Lead-based paints are being increasingly banned, but it's worth it to check the label – and run in the opposite direction if it says 'Lead'!
- **Formaldehyde:** A colourless and flammable gas that is used in building materials, textiles, and home goods, it exists within the human body, yet ingestion or exposure can affect several systems in the body, including the nervous, immune, respiratory and intestinal, and may also lead to cancer.
- **Bisphenol A (BPA):** This is an organic compound used to make plastics transparent, but it is highly toxic, affects the

endocrine system, and can also lead to obesity and cancer.

- **Volatile Organic Compounds (VOCs):** These compounds cause indoor air pollution. They are found in paints, glue and solvents used to coat surfaces, ethane from fossil fuels, and a host of other surfaces and chemicals used in homes or other indoor spaces.

SafeBook Quiz

Apart from lead, one other metal, which is, by the way, liquid at room temperature, is also highly toxic. Often found as a bright red liquid line in old-style thermometers, which metal is this? *Hint:* It's also called quicksilver.

21 WHAT'S IMPORTANT ABOUT CLOTHES TAGS?

There's a lot to read in the symbols on the labels stitched in your clothes. From how to care for them and make them last for long to information about washing, ironing, bleaching and dry-cleaning, these tags are stuffed with useful advice.

Quick List

Machine wash	Machine wash, permanent press	Machine wash, delicate	Hand wash	Do not wash	Bleach
Do not bleach	Non-chlorine bleach	Non-chlorine bleach	Water temperature 30°C	Water temperature 40°C	Water temperature 50°C
Water temperature 60°C	Water temperature 70°C	Water temperature 95°C	Iron	Do not iron	No steam
Water temperature 30°C	Water temperature 40°C	Water temperature 50°C	Water temperature 60°C	Water temperature 70°C	Water temperature 95°C
Low temperature	Medium temperature	High temperature	Tumble dry	Low heat	Medium heat
High heat	No heat	Permanent press	Delicate	Hang to dry	Drip dry
Short cycle	Reduced moisture	Low heat	No steam finishing	Dry	Dry flat

SafeBook Says

> Guess what? You can play the guessing game with clothes you already have or have just bought. Check the symbols on the tag and say what you think the symbol means. Then check! Did you get them all correct?

Section Three

ELECTRICITY

22 IS A 'SHORT CIRCUIT' REALLY A SHORT WIRE ON FIRE?

Short circuits are highly dangerous electrical situations. But no, they have nothing to do with the length of wire. A short circuit is related to the flow and the amount of electric current in the wires.

First things first. What is a circuit?
A circuit has:

1. electronic components
2. a power source

These are connected by a wire that provides a path through which current flows. When the current flows in a proper fashion, it meets components that use up electricity and reduce its strength. A short circuit happens if two wires that are *not* supposed to touch each other, bump into one another. This leads the current to surge through this *new* path in large amounts, causing the components and the wires to heat up excessively – this is what causes the fire.

To avoid short circuits

DO

- ☑ Make sure that all the wires are insulated properly. Cuts and tears in the wire can cause short circuits.
- ☑ Install fuses and circuit-breakers, which help eliminate the risk of short circuits. They are designed to break the current flow if they encounter a large amount of electric current, thereby reducing damage to the components.
- ☑ Unplug electrical and electronic gadgets when not in use.

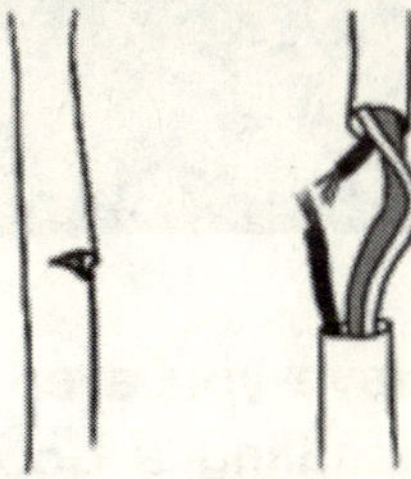

Wire with a cut (left) and a tear (right)

SafeBook Says

"According to the Mumbai Fire Brigade department, 80 per cent of fires are caused by short circuits."

23 WHAT HAPPENS WHEN YOU GET AN ELECTRIC SHOCK?

Have you ever felt a tingling sensation when handling a doorknob or handing over a pair of scissors? If yes, then you have already experienced harmless shock due to static electricity. Electric current is defined by the flow of tiny, charged particles called electrons. When these electrons move quickly through your body, you will get an electric shock.

Now, depending on the amount of current and the path it takes to flow through your body, the effects of shock can range from harmless jolts to a full-scale heart attack (cardiac arrest) or even death.

To avoid an electric shock:

DO

☑ Keep appliances away from water.

☑ Use three-prong plugs in your electrical sockets.

☑ Make sure that the power is turned off when fixing electrical and electronic equipment.

DON'T

☒ Touch an electrical outlet or switch with a wet hand.

☒ Ever touch a person getting an electric shock. If possible, have a grown-up switch off the main supply and use a wooden rod to break the contact between the person and supply.

SafeBook Says

"The most resistance in your body is in your skin. If your skin is wet or damp, that resistance is lowered. If you handle an electrical device with damp hands, even voltages under 20V or so (not enough to even light a low-wattage lamp) might be sufficient to do you serious damage."

24 WHAT ICONS TO LOOK FOR WHEN BUYING ELECTRONIC GOODS

Look closely at any packaging of electronic items. You will find maybe a dozen little widget-like icons. They are either warnings, disclaimers or proofs of safety. Why do we need them? Because the market is flooded with sub-standard appliances, faulty parts or poor-quality wiring. This could lead to overheating, or worse, shock or fire.

You would certainly have read about or seen mobile-phone chargers exploding or catching fire. So, would safe, certified, and tested electronic appliances be a good idea? You bet.

We also hope you are environment warriors, because we also need to consider environmental impact and how much electricity is guzzled.

SafeBook Says

"Never compromise on quality when it comes to electronic goods. No point in having a pretty, pink (but substandard) hairdryer if, one fine day, it could burn down your house, right?"

Luckily, now electronic goods come with icons that help you with your checklist.

Quick List

Double Insulation Double layer of insulation (like in a thermos flask) to prevent electric shocks; does not require a separate ground pin.	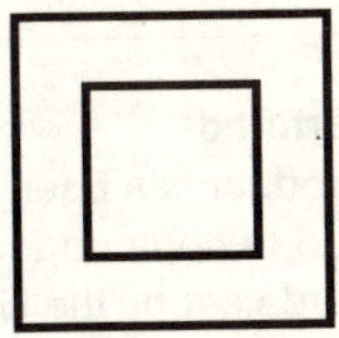
Indoor Use These products are meant to be kept inside the house only, and will get damaged if exposed to sun and outside air.	
WEEE Waste Electrical and Electronic Equipment Directive. The WEEE symbol asks for safe disposal, collection, and recycling of electronic waste. In short, do NOT dump WEEE products in a regular bin!	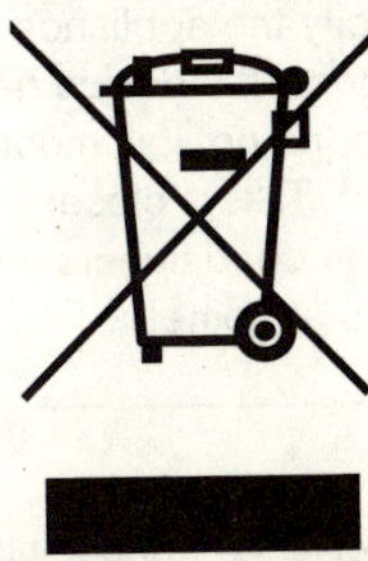
European Conformity This is a certification symbol. It means that the product meets safety, health, and environment standards in Europe. European certifying organizations are sticklers for safety.	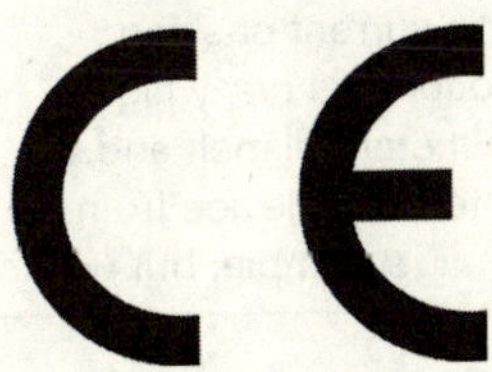

UL Certified Certified by Underwriters Laboratory, USA, to meet the safety regulations of your country.	
ISI Certified The product has been certified to conform to Indian standards set by the Bureau of Indian Standards.	
BEE Star Rating Set by the Bureau of Energy Efficiency (isn't BEE a cute acronym?), the label indicates how much electricity the appliance consumes. If a device gets a 5-star rating, it is most efficient. Take a closer look at the air conditioners and geysers at home!	
Fuse The appliance comes with an inbuilt strip of metal. If the current passing through it is crazy high, the metal will melt and will protect the device from damage. Simple, but works!	 IEC 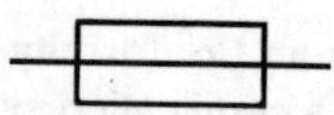 IEEE/ANSI  IEEE/ANSI

25 WHY SHOULD YOU HAVE MCBs IN YOUR HOUSE?

You must have heard your parents mention the MCB, which is an important, if usually hidden, device in every home. A house may use multiple MCBs – one for every unit or room of the house and a big one for the entire electricity supply.

MCB stands for Miniature Circuit Breaker. Let's break this down to understand. You have probably studied what a circuit is in your science class. Circuit breakers are devices that protect circuits from overload, that is, too much electric current. A fuse does the exact same job but, unlike a fuse which can be used only once and then needs to be replaced, MCBs can simply be reset. MCBs are also:

- more sensitive to overcurrent,
- and generally more expensive,
- but their components rarely need to be replaced,
- so they are cheaper in the long term.

MCBs are also safer since the user can't easily disable them. Even if, by error, a fuse of the wrong size is put, when the intensity of current increases or any device malfunctions, and an overload is caused, the house circuitry could catch fire. In such cases, MCBs can literally save the day.

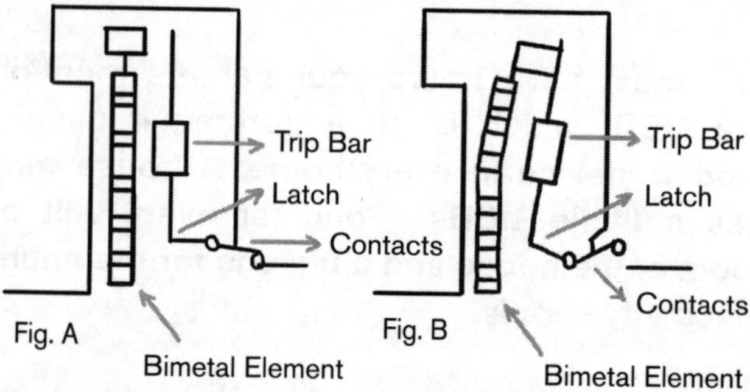

Quick Science

- An MCB has four important parts: a **bimetal element** (a fancy term for a strip containing two metals), a **trip bar**, a **latch** and **contacts**. When excess current flows through the MCB, the bimetal element gets heated and bends as shown in Fig. B.
- The latch is attached to the contacts. When the element bends, the latch is released.
- It then opens the MCB contacts, and the MCB 'trips' or turns off.
- The flow of the current is stopped, and the circuit gets protected.

- The MCB must be reset by manually turning it ON to restart the flow of current.
- Before resetting the circuit breaker, ALWAYS turn off or unplug the electronic devices that were being used when the breaker was activated – electricity in one phase or even the whole house could just blow.

SafeBook Says

What is the difference between a stabilizer and an MCB? A voltage stabilizer – that rather heavy and ugly box on walls near air conditioners, for instance – protects the appliance from voltage fluctuations – that's when the voltage increases or decreases, making the lights flicker or dim spookily. An MCB protects the appliance against overcurrent (excess flow of current) and short circuit. Listen carefully when you learn about electric circuits in physics class!

26 RUBBER SLIPPERS AND ELECTRICITY: A SAFE COMBO

You must have often heard grown-ups say that you must not interfere with any electric equipment without wearing slippers. What is it about rubber slippers that they are often recommended when repairing or handling electrical tools? The answer is simple. They are good insulators.

Not all objects around us are good at carrying electricity. The ones that are good at it, such as metals, are called *conductors* whereas the bad carriers of electricity are called *insulators*. Wood and rubber are the most common examples of insulators.

So, how exactly does a rubber slipper being an insulator help? Essentially, current flows from higher to lower potential and the ground is always the lowest. Thus, electric current tends to flow from the top of your body to your feet and then into the earth. A rubber slipper effectively blocks this connection between the feet and ground, and so prevents the person from getting an electric shock.

You may have seen electricians keeping one hand in their pocket when doing electrical repairs. That is good safety practice. Why? Because the path of the electric current from one hand to the other gets broken and the vital organs in the chest cavity are protected.

Let us look at the safe practices while handling electrical items:

DO

- ☑ Unplug the electrical appliance before you start to clean it.
- ☑ Keep electrical wires and appliance cords away from sources of heat.

DON'T EVER

- ☒ Use an appliance near a sink, bathtub or other source of water.
- ☒ Touch any electrical appliance or device, such as a light switch, hairdryer or toaster, if you are touching water.
- ☒ Use any electrical appliance if you are wet, like right after having a bath.

☒ Pull an electric plug out of the wall outlet by yanking on the electric cord.

SafeBook Quiz

Which naturally occurring element (that is, one that is not made in a lab) is the fastest conductor of electricity?

☐ A. Iron
☐ B. Silver
☐ C. Copper

27 WHAT ARE CHILD-PROOF SOCKETS?

Happens all the time: you want to plug your mobile charger (2-pin) in an electrical socket and you can't – something inside the socket pushes back. Why does this happen? It is very likely that there's a shutter inside the outlet that blocks the entrance of the two pins of your charger. And you end up sticking some sharp object into the third pin of the socket. Bad idea!

Such outlets are known as tamper-resistant (TR) outlets and they let you plug in only if the plug has a larger third pin known as the ground pin. As soon as this third pin is inserted, a spring mechanism inside the socket pushes aside the shutter and lifts the shutters for the two bottom pins. These outlets are also called child-proof sockets since they prevent small children, who might play with sockets and try to push

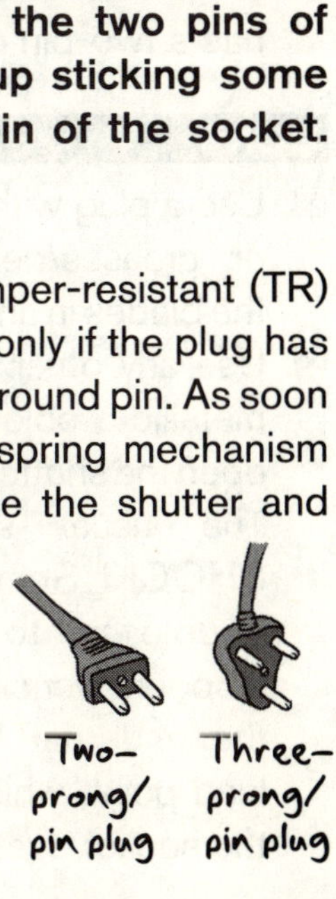

random objects into the sockets, from getting an electric shock.

DO

☑ Carefully straighten out the blades if a plug's blade is bent or splayed – this will help the pins fit better in the shutter.

☑ Please, please get it replaced if a plug is damaged and has a sharp edge or uneven tip. Inserting damaged plugs into sockets can only spell bad news.

☑ Use the ground pin of a three-pin plug to open the shutter and then plug in any appliance that has a two-pin plug in a three-pin socket.

DON'T

☒ Use a plug with cracks or creases/bends on the blades in any outlet.

☒ Use any other pointed metallic objects to open the shutter. Why? The usual suspect: SHOCK! Sometimes, people try to use a wooden pencil, using the end that has the lead point, which could snap and get stuck in the socket. Just DON'T do it!

SafeBook Says

> **Some outlets are designed to work with two pins as well. You just need to push the plug in straight, so that both pins hit the shutters at the same time.**

28 CAN YOU SAVE A PERSON FROM AN ELECTRIC SHOCK?

Thousands of people die every year of electric shock – mostly due to careless handling of electric equipment. This is tragic because this is a most preventable hazard, and it needs the very basic safety precautions.

Q1: What is an electric shock?
Q2: How does one get an electric shock?

A1: When too much electric current passes through the body, it gives a shock. A mild shock may simply give you a tingling sensation, but a strong one could kill you.

A2: When a human body comes in contact with a source of voltage that is high enough to cause current flow through the body.

Whenever you use an electronic product, make sure that you:

- Have read through the user manual carefully.
- Check the product for any loose wire ends and incorrect insulation.
- Follow all the safety precautions during use.

But what does high voltage current *do*? It can damage human tissues or cause fibrillation, which is a big word for making your heartbeat irregular. Electric shock can also cause death by electric current, or electrocution. Currents of about 100 mA (milliamperes) can be lethal when applied to the sensitive parts of the human body – that's usually the parts protected by your ribcage, such as the heart and lungs.

The thing is, mistakes happen, and people can suffer from a shock. What should you or shouldn't you do then?

DO

☑ Turn off the main supply of power either by tripping the MCB, fuse box or the main switch.

☑ Get a grown-up to use an insulating material such as things made of wood, cardboard or paper to separate the person from the current source if you cannot turn off the power or don't know where the fuse box is, but **DO NOT** use a wet cloth.

☑ Check the person for injuries or burns and make a note for the doctor.

☑ Have the person checked-up by a doctor, and this is an absolute must in severe cases of electric shock.

DON'T

- ☒ Touch the person if they are still in contact with the current source; call an ambulance instead.
- ☒ Abandon the poor shock victim. Wait for help or the ambulance to arrive.

SafeBook Says

"The minimum current that a human can feel is 1 milliampere (mA). A shock of more than 200 mA is so strong that a person's heart can literally stop beating."

29 WHAT TO DO (OR NOT DO) WITH ELECTRICAL CABLES

Most electrical fires are caused by faulty electrical outlets and outdated appliances. Other fires are started by faults in appliance cords, sockets and switches. Checking these beforehand and from time to time is the best thing you can do.

In simple terms, electricity produces heat. When it goes crazy, it can cause a HUGE amount of damage. Using an appliance with a worn or frayed cord that can send heat on to wooden floors, furniture, curtains and rugs, is like asking for trouble.

Which brings us to cables. Cables do the job of carrying electricity from the power source to, well, anywhere, so they need to be in tip-top condition as well as handled with utmost care. They need to be placed out of reach of small children and pets, and checked regularly for signs of damage.

Quick List

- Never run your cords under a rug or a carpet. Current generates heat and under a carpet, it cannot escape. The trapped heat could cause an electrical fire.

- If an appliance has a 3-pin plug, NEVER remove the third prong. That extra prong is NOT for show; it is the ground pin, which helps the appliance draw extra electricity.*
- Outdated wiring often causes electrical fires. If a home is over 20 years old, it may not have the wiring capacity to handle the amount of electricity required by the hundreds of appliances we now use, like laptops, wide-screen and smart TVs, video and gaming players, microwave ovens and air conditioners.
- Possibly the worst and most dangerous thing to do with electric wires is to connect equipment to the socket without a plug, directly through live wires. Electric cables have a plastic covering, which is insulating material (as opposed to combustible). A wire directly connected into the socket can really magnify the chances of getting an electric shock.

* *See 'Why Is Removing the Ground Pin from a Plug not a Good Idea?'*

- Lastly, extension cords are useful to plug in lots of appliances but remember: the power outlet is just one, so your appliances can get overheated and blow. All those tangled cables could also cause an electrical fire. Extension cords are an *emergency measure*. The moment you realize that you need all the extra sockets, call in an electrician and get new ones installed right on the wall.*

SafeBook Quiz

Let's say you find that the plastic casing of your TV cord has a cut and the live wire is exposed. What do you do?

- ☐ A. Patch it up with normal sticking tape.
- ☐ B. Patch it up with electrical tape.
- ☐ C. Replace the wire completely.
- ☐ D. Leave it be since a minor cut is not dangerous.

** See 'What to Do or not Do with Electrical Cables'*

30 WHY IS REMOVING THE GROUND PIN FROM A PLUG NOT A GOOD IDEA?

It sounds weird, but some people actually remove the third pin of a three-pronged plug to fit it in a regular two-pin socket. Just so you know, the ground pin is there to save your life.

Let us first see what grounding means.

Grounding or earthing is a method to transmit instant electricity directly to the ground via electrical cables. Even if a device is not properly insulated, grounding allows an overflow of electricity to literally go into the ground and prevent electrocution. The principle of grounding is simple: if electric current escapes from a device, it will get diverted to a metallic conductor (cable) that ends with a stake (rod) buried in the ground. Don't scoff – these things happen. Losses of current may occur, for example, when a damaged power cable is stripped and the electrical wires come into contact with the device's casing.

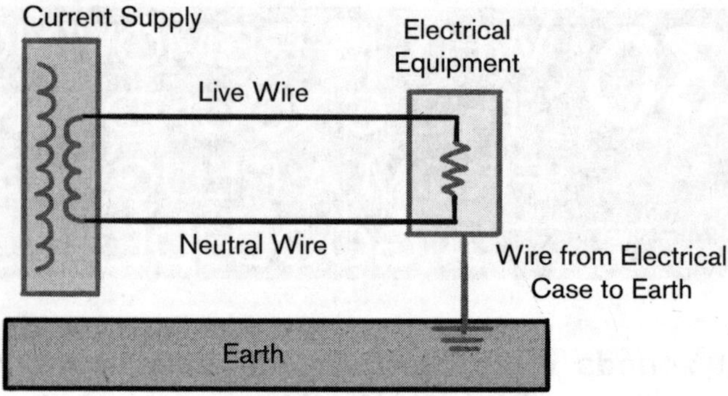

How earthing works

Quick Science

In an electrical circuit, there are three kinds of wires:

Red: The live wire, which carries the current from the power source to the equipment;

Black: A neutral wire, which carries the current from the equipment back to the source; and

Green: A ground wire, which connects the equipment to the ground.

Easy so far? Let's go on.

The ground is considered to be at zero potential. Now electric current always flows from the higher potential to the lower potential. So, any excess current would directly flow to the lowest potential, i.e., the ground, through the ground wire.

If there is a failure in the appliance with this type of plug, the third pin, which also reduces electrical noise, will create a short circuit and blow the breaker or fuse.

And what's electrical noise? It is a humming or buzzing sound that occurs because there is an unwanted electrical signal that interferes with an electrical device, especially one whose cables carry signals or data. Printers, for example, have high electrical noise as they get heated up, and can slow down other signals. Electrical noise cannot be completely removed, but grounding can help reduce, or minimize it, to quite an extent.

Without this pin to turn off the power on the short-circuited device, the current will electrocute the user. Good enough reason to NOT tamper with the ground pin!

SafeBook Says

A lightning conductor is a device that works on the same principle. The conducting rod placed at the top of buildings is connected to a metal plate buried in the ground and thus transmits any electrical discharge from the atmosphere directly to the ground and makes the building safe. Look out for lightning conductor strips running vertically along buildings, but DO NOT TOUCH THEM!

31 USING AN IMMERSION ROD TO HEAT WATER

An immersion rod is an electric appliance that is dipped into water in a bucket or a tub to heat water. Doesn't it already sound dangerous? Still, people do use it when they don't have any other water-heating device.

The immersion rod contains a coated metal rod that kind of hangs in a container of water. When the power is switched on, electric current passing through the rod causes it to heat up and the water into which it has been dipped also heats up.

The golden rule: water and electricity DO NOT mix. The problem is that immersion rods are readily available, and they are cheap as compared to geysers. But if there's even a slight fault in the rod, electrical current will leak into the water and can lead to a severe shock. If there's no choice but to use one, make sure that you buy the best quality and the most reliable immersion heater available in the market.

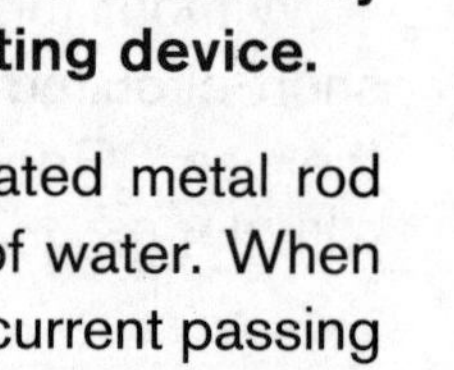

DO

☑ Be careful of burns; water heated by an immersion rod can get too hot and can scald your body severely.

DON'T

☒ Use the rod in a plastic bucket with very little water as this could cause the bucket to melt.

☒ Touch the water being heated while the rod is switched on, never, ever! You WILL get a horrible shock.

☒ Switch on the rod before dipping it into water.

☒ Touch the water 'to check if the rod is on'. Switch off the power, count slowly to 10 and then check.

☒ Use the immersion heater in a metal bucket as this can directly cause electric shocks.

SafeBook Quiz

Does distilled water conduct electricity?

A. Yes, water itself is a good conductor of electricity.

B. No, because it does not contain any impurity.

32 WHAT TO DO IF A LIVE ELECTRIC LINE FALLS ON THE ROAD

If you ever come across a live electrical wire, lying in your path, STAY AWAY FROM IT. These electric lines carry a great deal of electricity and are potentially capable of energizing the ground as well, making that patch of ground capable of giving a shock.

Although insulators are poor carriers of electricity, it doesn't mean they can't carry electricity. In the case of electric cables that carry electricity to homes and other places, the voltage is so high that even insulators like wood might not be safe. You should also avoid touching any object in contact with it.

DO

☑ Keep away from power lines if you are flying a kite. Kite or balloon strings tangled in power lines can be dangerous: electricity can travel down the line and cause a shock or start a fire.

☑ Stay at least **10 feet away** from any wet surface or swimming pool if you are operating an electrical tool, using an electrical appliance or playing with an electrical toy outside.

☑ Have an adult call the power company to report the downed wire immediately. You should avoid touching the wire, even with a stick.

☑ In case a power line falls on your car, stay inside the car as the ground outside may be energized. Do not step out unless the fire department and power company workers tell you to do so. When leaving the car, jump straight out of the car, with both arms close to your sides, to avoid touching the car when your feet hit the ground.

DON'T

☒ Climb trees that are near power lines or have power lines running through them.

☒ Ever try to remove the item from the power lines yourself if you see something stuck or tangled in a power line. Have an adult call the power company.

- ☒ Ever touch a power line with any part of your body or any object.
- ☒ Ever fly model aeroplanes or remote-controlled aeroplanes or helicopters near overhead power lines. Play with them in open areas such as parks or fields.
- ☒ Ever go into an electric substation for any reason. If a pet has wandered off into the area, do not try to get it yourself. Have an adult call the power company.
- ☒ Touch any electrical tools, appliances or toys if you are wet, standing in a puddle or are in a pool.

SafeBook Says

"You must have seen birds sitting on power lines. Do you know why they don't get electric shocks? Hint: It has something to do with grounding."

SafeBook Quiz

Why do birds perching on electrical wires never get electrocuted?

33 CAN YOU SAFELY PUT MANY PLUGS INTO A SINGLE OUTLET?

Around festivals and other celebrations, the electrical outlet usually begins to put on extra weight, doesn't it? There are strings of lights, speakers, electric candles, what have you, and wires snaking around everywhere, overloading the outlet – and the result can be dangerous.

So, how many things can you plug into an outlet before it will catch fire? Let's do a little math. The formula looks like this:

P/E=I or P/V=I where Power (in watts) divided by Electromotive Force or Voltage (volts) equals Intensity of Current (amperes)

Say you're using 3,500 watts (W) of power with your holiday lights and other decorations. Divide 3,500 by the number of volts at home (220 in India) and what do you get? 16 amperes (amps or A for short) of current. The electrical points in most homes can allow 5 or 15 amps. So the circuit in your 15-amp outlet is overloaded. Result? It could be a fire!

Ideally, you should only use 80 per cent of the current that an electrical outlet is designed for – so in this case you need a 20-amp outlet – that simply means you need more than one socket.

DO

- ☑ Always check the rating of the electrical outlet before you start plugging in appliances.
- ☑ The math using the formula above, after checking the labels on the device to see how much power they draw.
- ☑ Remember, heavy appliances like air conditioners, refrigerators, geysers, and similar electrical equipment should be plugged in separately and that outlet should not have any other equipment plugged into it. An air conditioner, in particular, draws a lot of power, so a separate MCB switch is recommended.
- ☑ Use extension cords sparingly and only as a temporary solution. In case you need different kinds of equipment plugged in for longer periods, get an outlet installed by an electrician.

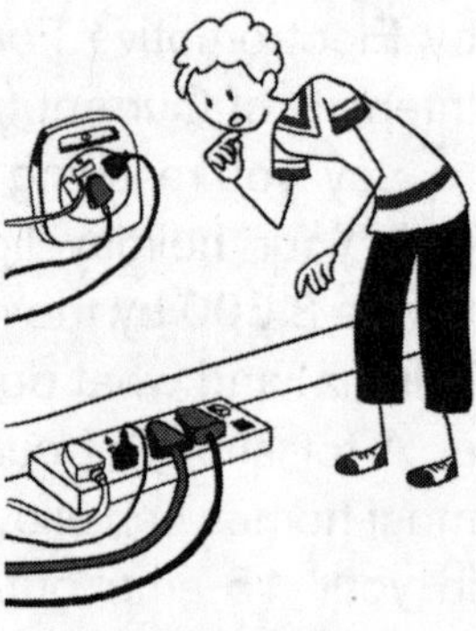

DON'T

- ☒ Ever plug the heavy-power–drawing appliances on an extension cord; they are not designed to handle that kind of load.
- ☒ Ever use an extension cord in another extension cord to plug in more devices. This is SUPER dangerous and can lead to a short circuit or an electrical overload.

SafeBook Says

"Generally, appliances such as televisions, music systems, computers, mixers and electric irons are all rated below 1000 W. So, you should use 5-amp outlets for all these. For heavy loads such as air conditioners, water heaters, refrigerators and inverter sockets, you need to use 15-amp outlets as they draw power of around 3000 W."

34 WHAT TO DO IN CASE OF A POWER OUTAGE

We have all faced a power outage or a power cut. It happens if a storm occurs, a power line has fallen, or the local transformer has malfunctioned. In some areas, production of electricity does not meet public demand, and so there are scheduled power cuts.

When an outage occurs, first check to see if the power failure is all over the neighbourhood and not just in your home. If others around you have electricity, your MCB or fuse panel could have a problem. If the entire neighbourhood is plunged into darkness, call the power company to notify them. Prolonged power outage is a nuisance, but here are some dos and don'ts as preparation:

DO

☑ Turn off all appliances, in fact, unplug them (this is a MUST during a thunderstorm) so that when the power comes back, the sudden surge in current doesn't damage appliances.

☑ Keep one or two lights switched on so that when the power is restored, you'll know ☺!

☑ In case you must use a candle, make sure it is always under adult supervision, and ensure that it is placed away from anything that can catch fire (curtains, tablecloths, clothes, books). Battery-operated emergency lights are a much safer option in the situation than candles.

☑ Keep the electricity usage to a minimum if you have inverter backup: it could get overloaded or even run out before the regular power supply is restored.

DON'T

☒ Open your fridge or freezer unless necessary. Opening the fridge frequently will affect the cold temperature environment inside.

☒ Ever use a power generator indoors. It emits toxic gases, which can cause health problems. It should always be kept outdoors and ideally kept 20 feet away from windows.

SafeBook Quiz

What is the toxic gas produced by generators? Being colourless and odourless, it can go undetected and lead to severe respiratory and health problems.

35 WHY DO BATTERIES EXPLODE?

In today's world, especially since the COVID-19 pandemic, laptops, mobiles, tablets and what-not have made us all 'power' hungry. Devices need to have a great battery life and need to work for hours on a single charge. So, manufacturers have tried to make devices more and more compact, yet power-packed.

These batteries run a very real risk of overheating and eventually exploding. While most devices nowadays use lithium ion (Li-ion) batteries, other common types include nickel-cadmium and lead acid, among others.

Why do batteries explode? First let's see how batteries work.

Quick Science

- Every battery has two electrodes (conductors): the positively charged cathode and the negatively charged anode. They are dipped in chemicals known as electrolytes.

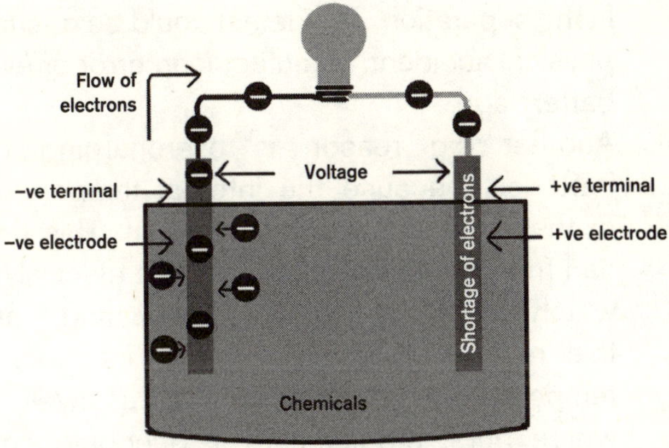

How a battery works

- When the battery is used, electrons from the anode flow towards the cathode via these electrolytes. The flow of current powers your device.
- With time, the anode keeps losing electrons, as it keeps supplying them to the cathode as you use your device and, eventually, your battery dies.
- In rechargeable batteries, this flow is reversed while the device is charging, so electrons flow from the cathode to the anode.
- The cathode and anode are kept separated by a thin layer to prevent direct flow between them, since the reaction between them would be rapid and could lead to an explosion. A major cause of battery explosions is a defect

in the separation. The defect could be due to a physical accident, manufacturing error or even battery age.

- Another big reason is overcharging the batteries, because the internal temperature of the battery increases due to it. This heat can trigger a chain reaction in the electrolyte, which then causes rapid heating, and this results in an uncontrolled increase in temperature. The battery could thus swell, or worse, burst into flames. This phenomenon is called 'thermal runaway'.

So, what's the right thing to do? Easy as pie. *Use a certified charger.* It provides controlled current flow and even restricts this flow to the battery once the phone gets charged. If you use uncertified, untested chargers, your battery life decreases and risk of explosion increases.

SafeBook Quiz

Who is credited with the invention of the electric battery? (*Hint*: The unit for potential is named after him.)

36 HOW TO HANDLE BULBS

We use all kinds of light fixtures: old-style bulbs (called incandescent bulbs), compact fluorescent lamps (CFLs), tube lights and light-emitting diodes (LEDs). Each lamp comes with a power rating called wattage and a voltage specification, usually given at the base of the bulb.

The higher the wattage,
the brighter the light from the bulb, and
the more the electricity it will consume.

Incandescent bulbs contain a thin wire, called a filament, made of the element tungsten, which resists the flow of current. When electricity passes through the filament, its resistance makes it heat up so much so that it starts glowing and producing light. The bulb can get extremely hot, and if you go near it, you can feel the radiated heat.

Changing a light bulb is easy and you don't need to be an electrician to do it, but do remember the following points:

DO

☑ Be careful of a few things: if you apply too much force, the bulb can break, and a broken bulb may contain harmful chemicals (CFLs contain mercury, which is *very toxic*!).

DON'T

☒ Ever use a vacuum cleaner to clean up the broken fragments of a bulb, especially CFLs. The mercury powder or vapour will spread by the vacuuming action, and that is very, very dangerous to ingest.

Quick Tips

- Incandescent bulbs produce more heat than light, so keep them away from any flammable material.
- Match the wattage and voltage specifications of the bulb to the holder or fitting. Incorrect specifications can lead to electrical fires.
- Changing a bulb? Bravo! But turn its switch off first. Hold the bulb/CFL/LED lightly and then place in the holder. Gently rotate the bulb so that it is locked in the holder or screwed on properly.
- If you break a bulb, especially a CFL, open all the windows and vacate the room for 15 minutes – allow the toxic chemicals to escape. Then, carefully scoop up the glass fragments

(*not* with your bare hands, please!) and place them in a sealed plastic bag. You can use sticky tape or dough to remove glass fragments. Mop the area well! You really do NOT want to step on broken-glass shards!

- If the bulb has the WEEE bin sign with a cross, it should be disposed of as e-waste, otherwise throw it in the regular trash, but do inform your garbage collector, else they could cut themselves on the glass while handling the trash. Wash your hands thoroughly after cleaning.

SafeBook Says

Light is generated either through incandescence (as in the case of the bulbs described above), which is a combination of light and heat, or luminescence, which is light without heat. There are many examples of luminescence, like bioluminescence (fireflies, light-emitting frogs, and so on), fluorescence (tube lights) and phosphorescence (glow-in-the-dark materials). Luminescence is measured by a unit called Candela.

37 HOW TO GET RID OF E-WASTE?

Tech products are becoming smarter and smarter, but their lifespans are getting shorter and shorter. Since we all want to have the latest and most cutting-edge gadgets, e-waste – that's electronic waste – is getting generated in large quantities.

Let's list a few e-waste items: mobile phones, laptops, desktops, hard disks, televisions, video game consoles, stereos, microwaves, heaters, electric cookers, remote controls, smart watches... oh goodness, the list just doesn't end, does it?

Okay now, what's the deal with electronic gadgets? Firstly, they contain valuable materials like gold, silver, platinum, palladium and copper, which can be reclaimed – and reused – by recycling. But, but, but. They also contain toxic materials – lead, mercury, cadmium, beryllium, PVC plastics and other chemicals.

If they are dumped in regular trash, they are likely to be burnt. The fumes from burning e-waste can cause bad respiratory problems. The burnt stuff can leach into the soil and contaminate the groundwater. So, the environment gets harmed for sure, and moreover, our brain, heart, liver, kidneys, and the nervous system can all get pretty badly affected. Better watch all that e-waste!

Quick Tips

- First thing. Do you, like, really need that new device? Sure, go ahead and buy if it's really essential. The easiest way to not generate e-waste is to not buy stuff that will end up as such.
- Buying a new phone? Exchange your old phone. Let it get recycled!
- Sell off your old electronic gadgets before they fall apart completely – enough people and organizations can make use of them.
- Even better… donate your old electronic equipment while it's still safely usable to NGOs for the use of students or less privileged people. Do a good deed.

SafeBook Says

"Have you noticed a bin symbol with a cross on your smartphone's box? That's the WEEE or Waste Electrical and Electronic Equipment Directive symbol that classifies the product to be treated as e-waste once discarded."

- Don't know whom to offer or sell your old stuff? Call or visit a service centre. They usually have schemes. Manufacturers themselves have e-waste management schemes. Get on the Internet for a good cause!

Section Four

ON THE ROAD

38 WHAT SAFETY FEATURES DOES A CAR HAVE?

Well, of course you know about seat belts being a safety feature. But do you know that cars today come equipped with a whole lot of features to safeguard passengers?

Car safety features can be categorized into two types: active and passive. Active safety systems help to avoid accidents and passive ones aid in reducing the effects of accidents. Look at the safety features listed below. Which ones do you think are active, and which ones, passive? Write P (for Passive) and A (for Active) in the box against the names.

Quick List

☐ 1. **Laminated Windshield:** This type of windshield is like a glass sandwich. Two 'slices' of laminated, shatter-proof glass are stuck together with a layer of plastic in between. So, if an accident occurs, they do not break into shards but into many harmless chunks that stay stuck to the plastic.

- ☐ 2. **Airbags:** In case of a collision (that's when the car bangs into some other vehicle or a hard object), airbags inflate like balloons and cushion the passenger so they don't hit the dashboard, steering wheel or windshield. Side airbags reduce the risk of occupants hitting the door or objects that crash through it.
- ☐ 3. **Anti-lock Braking System (ABS):** When a car driver applies the brake suddenly, the tyres can skid and make the driver lose control of the car. ABS reduces the risk of tyres skidding under heavy braking and allows the driver to maintain control of the car. ABS only operates under heavy braking or on slippery surfaces.
- ☐ 4. **Crumple Zones:** A car has three parts: the front, the passenger compartment and the rear. In a collision, the impact can harm passengers inside it. The front and rear parts are designed so that they crumple like paper. This absorbs most of the impact and reduces the brunt on the passengers.
- ☐ 5. **Seat Belts:** When a moving car stops suddenly, the body will keep moving forward and can hit the steering wheel, dashboard or windshield. In case of a crash, seat belts

will keep you in your place and reduce the risk of injury from these parts of the car.

☐ 6. **Mirrors:** When the side and rear-view mirrors are properly aligned, the driver can see better all round, and this eliminates, or minimizes, the dangerous blind spot.

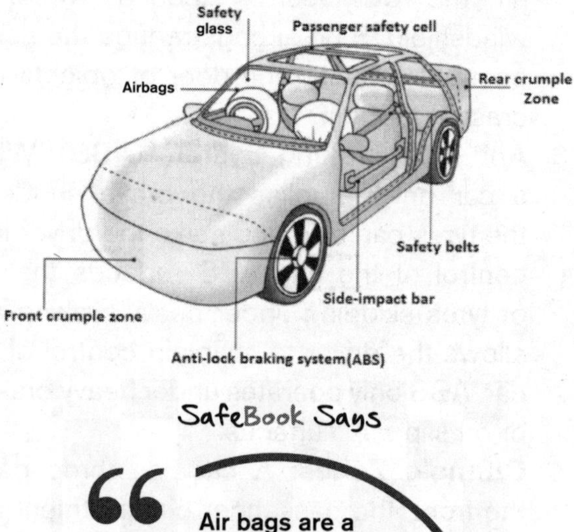

SafeBook Says

> Air bags are a complementary safety feature, i.e., they work in combination with the seat belt. When air bags get inflated during a collision, the passenger should be belted, else the sudden impact of the inflation could be fatal. So make sure everyone in the car is belted up!

39 OUT IN THE RAIN?

Weather can affect traffic. Being on the road in the rain can be very challenging due to reduced visibility and steering ability.

On top of this, strong winds may cause falling/fallen debris on the road and vehicles will need to navigate carefully to avoid this. Vulnerable road users such as pedestrians, cyclists and motorcyclists need to be allowed extra space to avoid the mud, puddles, or slippery parts of the road. Make sure you tell the driver to keep the following points in mind.

Quick Tips

- Wet roads do not offer enough traction (meaning **grip**, so skidding is a real threat). Speeding the vehicle can cause the tyre to slip and result in an accident.

SafeBook Says

> **"On a road filled with water, the force on a vehicle is only due to the water, but the pressure felt by the driver depends on the vehicle as well."**

- Avoid sudden braking or the vehicle could skid.
- Try not to drive on roads with moving water; water could enter the fuel tank or other parts and damage them.
- Use defrosters to prevent condensation on the windshield and increase visibility.
- Stay at a good distance from other vehicles as it can take ten times longer for a vehicle to respond to brakes on a wet or flooded road.
- Keep your headlights on so that you are visible to other drivers.

SafeBook Says

"*The science*: Pressure and force are related. The equation is Pressure (P) = Force (F)/Area (A). So, for the same amount of force, the pressure felt by the driver depends on the area of contact as well."

SafeBook Quiz

Assume that water exerts 2,000 units of pressure. Tyres of Vehicle A cover 50 units of area in water, while tyres of Vehicle B cover 200 units of area in water. Which vehicle driver feels less pressure due to water?

40 DRIVING IN HOT WEATHER?

India is a hot country for the most part, and summer driving can present some special challenges. Hot weather can severely affect a car and its performance. Most of the breakdowns happen due to overheating of vehicles. Hot weather puts additional strain on the battery and engine, and worse, the tyres are also more likely to get punctured. If the vehicle is not properly maintained, its safety is compromised.

If you and your family decide to take a road trip in the summer:

DO

- ☑ Wear and carry sunscreen and a hat or a scarf to protect you from the heat.
- ☑ Make sure that you or someone else in the car is carrying a fully charged mobile phone and some cash for emergencies.
- ☑ Check that pressure in your tyres is as required (tip: the correct tyre pressure for your car is

usually printed on the rim of the driver-side door). Under-inflated tyres can cause more heat build-up and can burst. Always carry a spare, called a stepney.

- ☑ Get the coolant in your radiator periodically replaced.
- ☑ Open a downwind window slightly for ventilation to avoid carbon monoxide poisoning if you get stuck on the road.

DON'T

- ☒ Try to remove the radiator cap when your car is hot, and do not pour water over a hot radiator or engine when driving in extreme heat. Wait for the engine to cool.
- ☒ Leave a child or pet (or anyone, for that matter!) in a parked car in extremely warm weather.

SafeBook Says

> **"Cars can heat up quickly. If your car doesn't have air conditioning and you are parked in the hot sun, if you don't open the windows, the temperatures inside the car can reach more than 50°C in just a few minutes."**

41 DO YOU KNOW YOUR BLIND SPOTS?

It's unlikely you have ever thought about this – blind spots are areas that a driver cannot see while driving. Yes, they exist! Make sure whoever is driving you knows about them too!

Let's do a little experiment. What letters do you see in this box?

R	L

Genius! So the R stands for Right and the L stands for Left. Just for a lark, sit about 2 feet from the book, close your right eye, stare at L and bring the book closer to you, bit by bit. Did you get it? At one point, R vanishes, *pfft*! That's your blind spot. Try the opposite eye and letter too!

On the road, the blind spot is the area around the vehicle that cannot be seen properly by the driver of that vehicle. Knowing about blind spots can help you avoid serious accidents, especially:

- When you are on a multi-lane road
- When the driver has to switch lanes
- When you take your vehicle out of parking

All vehicles have blind spots, larger vehicles have larger blind spots – here's a great reason to have a small car, hah! Side and rear-view mirrors need to be nicely aligned – *please* do not use them to look at yourself – as this helps the driver see better and eliminates or at least reduces the dangerous blind spots. To understand blind spots better, look at this image:

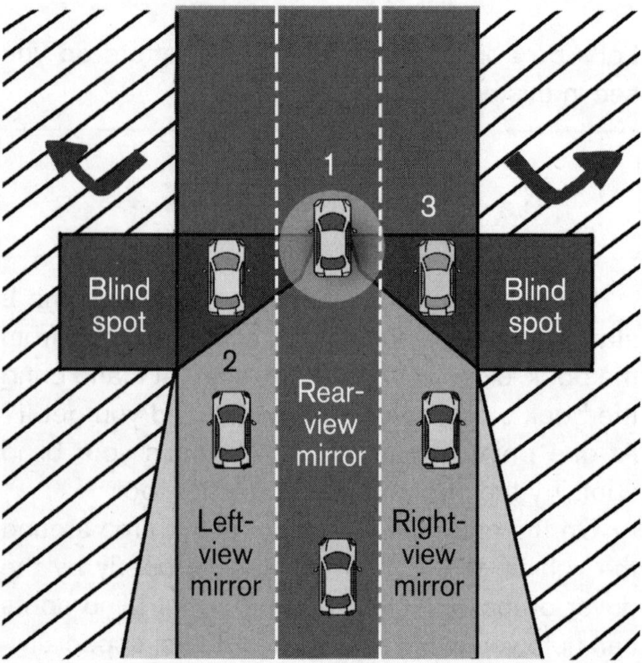

The lighter-grey-coloured areas shows the area that cannot be directly seen by the driver but can only be seen through the rear- and side-view mirrors. And even then, the driver of Car 1 will only be able to see Car 2 but not Car 3. Warning! Car 3 lies in the blind spot. So, if the driver wants to move over, they need to do a quick physical check over the shoulder, just to check and ensure there are no other vehicles around the car. More importantly, try not to be in the blind spots of other cars.

To avoid blind spots:

DO

☑ Check that the passenger-side side-view mirror is opened. Many drivers in India are reluctant to use it, but it is a safety device, not a cosmetic one.

☑ Be smart as a passenger: check to ensure that no child or animal is around the car when setting off. Also check for dogs under the car as they often take shelter there to escape the summer heat.

☑ Be careful when riding a bicycle near any moving vehicle; stay in an area that lies within the mirror view of the driver – and hope that the mirror is properly aligned!

☑ Adjust the rear-view mirror so that it covers the view straight out the rear window. It should not be tilted to one side, that's what the *side*-view mirrors are for!

☑ Remember to adjust the side-view mirror on the passenger side and check with the driver that they can see vehicles coming up from that side.

DON'T

☒ Play around any parked vehicle – if it starts when you are in the blind spot, you could get seriously hurt.

SafeBook Says

> "Nowadays, some cars are equipped with blind-spot monitors. These are sensor devices attached to the car's side and rear that send out either electronic or electromagnetic waves, or take images with a digital camera and notify the driver if any car gets close. How cool is that! Technology rules and keeps us safe to boot."

42 DO YOU HAVE TO CATCH A BUS TO SCHOOL?

Did you know that the 10-15 foot area around the bus is called the danger zone? If you take a bus, you should remain out of this area until the bus has come to a complete stop.

Besides being aware of the danger zone, you also need to be a good passenger so that the bus driver is not distracted. Here's what to keep in mind when catching a bus to school:

DO

- ☑ Always arrive at the bus stop five minutes before the scheduled arrival of the bus.
- ☑ Take your seat promptly and sit facing forward at all times.
- ☑ Place bags under your seat or on your lap.
- ☑ Remember to always keep the aisle space clear.
- ☑ Always keep your head, hands and arms inside the bus.
- ☑ Remain seated until the bus stops when you arrive at your destination. Use the handrails to get down. Take three or four big steps away from the bus to get out of the danger zone.
- ☑ Follow the driver's instructions.

DON'T

- ☒ Stand in the danger zone of the bus while you wait for the bus. If you need to cross the road to get on the bus, wait for the bus to stop and make sure that the driver sees you.
- ☒ Throw litter inside or outside the bus.
- ☒ Disturb the driver.

SafeBook Says

"Whenever you get on or off the bus, make eye contact with driver. It's simple: by making eye contact, you can see the driver and the driver can see you! In India, there is usually a conductor on the bus, so make sure the conductor knows you are getting off the bus."

43 HOW TO BECOME A SAFE CYCLIST

On the road, after pedestrians, cyclists are the most vulnerable, which means they are at risk. As fuel-powered traffic usually moves much faster than any bicycle, cyclists should diligently follow traffic rules and invest in gears and other instruments to ensure their complete safety.

QUICK TIPS

- Start by choosing a bicycle that best suits your needs and physical condition, including height and weight.
- Before buying your own new bicycle, borrow a friend's cycle, or make use of public cycles, if available. Your purchase will be an informed one.
- Always check the condition of your bicycle – tyre pressure, brakes, handlebar alignment and seat height – before riding it outside.
- Make sure that you plan your route in advance so that you have an idea of the traffic you could be dealing with on that road.

When you are out cycling:

DO

- ☑ Always wear a helmet while riding. Additional protective gear such as cycling gloves, and knee and elbow pads are also recommended.
- ☑ Wear light- and bright-coloured clothing when riding during the day and retroreflective/ fluorescent vests when riding at night.
- ☑ Ride on the left side of the road, always. When riding in a group, ride in a single file instead of riding parallel to each other.
- ☑ Obey all traffic lights and signals, and give proper hand signals.
- ☑ Maintain enough distance between you and the vehicle in front you, always. Enough distance means far enough so that if the vehicle in front brakes suddenly, you do not bump headlong into it, and have enough time to brake yourself.

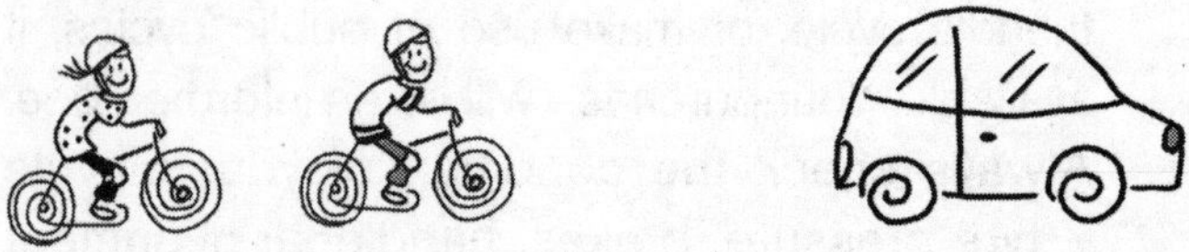

- ☑ Use a white front light and red rear light when riding at night or in poor visibility conditions.

☑ Apply the rear brake before the front brake when braking. The rear brake helps in gradual slowing down whereas the front brake is more abrupt and is to be used only when the front wheel is straight.

☑ Carry only light items when cycling, and use a bicycle bag.

DON'T

☒ Use the phone or earphones while riding, ever; we repeat, please stay alert on the road at all times!

☒ Carry any goods that may upset your balance.

SafeBook Says

"Two-wheeler users account for as much as 40 per cent of deaths in road accidents according to the data from the National Crime Records Bureau (2020)."

44 DO YOU REALLY KNOW HOW TO WALK ON THE ROAD?

Whether you are going to school or walking down to a friend's house or to the neighbourhood park, you may need to cross the road. A person who walks on the road is called a pedestrian, and as a pedestrian, you need to be extra careful on the road. So, how to be safe? Remember to stop, look, and listen.

SafeBook Asks

Always walk on sidewalks (footpaths). Sometimes, there may not be a footpath or roadside hawkers may have occupied it. In such situations, please walk on the right side of the road. Guess why – tick the answer you think is right from the options below, and then check.

☐ (a) Because India drives on the right side of the road.

☐ (b) So that you can hail a lift without difficulty.

☐ (c) So that you are able to see oncoming traffic.

As a pedestrian, keep the following things in mind on the road:

DO

- ☑ Use pedestrian crossings such as zebra crossings, overhead bridges and subways when crossing the road.
- ☑ Be alert to oncoming traffic. If there is an official gap in the median, look right, then left, then right again and cross quickly.
- ☑ Make sure that drivers in moving cars can see you clearly.
- ☑ Be visible. If you are on the road at night, try to wear bright, neon-coloured clothing, especially if you are walking in areas with poor lighting.
- ☑ Keep your eyes and ears open when crossing the road.

DON'T

- ☒ Cross the road if there is a median.

> SafeBook Says
>
> **"Pedestrian accidents are a major safety concern worldwide. About one-tenth of all traffic-related fatalities (deaths) involve a pedestrian. According to the data from the National Crime Records Bureau, more than 15,000 pedestrians lost their lives in 2016."**

- ☒ Step out on to the road in front of, or behind, a parked car as the driver could start the car and if you are in a blind spot, the driver would not be able to see you. If you absolutely must walk out into the road, stay in front of the car and make sure the driver has seen you.
- ☒ Stroll, look at your phone or use earphones when you are crossing the road and, above all, *never stop in the middle of the road*!

45 ARE YOU A GOOD PASSENGER?

A car has a driver, and you are the passenger. Who do you think is responsible for avoiding an accident on the road? The driver? Right. And what about you, the passenger? You are equally responsible!

You may ride pillion on a two-wheeler, or be a passenger in a cycle rickshaw, autorickshaw, car, van or bus. As a passenger, your job is to:

- Allow the driver to concentrate on driving the vehicle.
- Be helpful and support the driver so that you reach your destination safely.

To become a good passenger, follow the rules below:

DO

☑ Support the driver by offering to help navigate and keeping the music level appropriate. Ensure that the other passengers do not distract the driver.

- ☑ Be attentive on the road and see when the driver needs to be extra careful. Help the driver focus by pausing the conversation for a while or turning off the music.
- ☑ Ask the driver to slow down in a loud, clear voice if you feel the vehicle is going too fast.
- ☑ Offer the driver water and talk to them: it helps them keep awake and alert, particularly if it is a long drive and/or the driver has been at the wheel for a long time at unusual hours (also see the list of don'ts).
- ☑ Wear your seat belt at all times.
- ☑ Tap the driver's shoulder if you are slipping off the pillion seat on a motorcycle, and calmly tell them to stop so you can adjust yourself on the seat.

DON'T

- ☒ Turn on the lights inside the car at night: this could affect the driver's vision.
- ☒ Fall asleep and snore like a steam engine, please! A visibly (and audibly) sleeping passenger can trigger drowsiness in the driver too.

SafeBook Says

"Make sure that the driver is not looking at a phone while driving. Two seconds on a phone means driving blind for 33 metres."

46 WHAT'S THE BIG DEAL ABOUT ROAD SIGNS?

Road signs are seen on the edges of the road. They are put up by the government to help people use the road safely and to prevent road accidents. When people apply for a driver's licence, they need to take a test to demonstrate that they can identify and obey all the necessary traffic signs. A road sign tells you to do one of three things:

1. It tells you what to do (Order).
2. It gives you a warning (Caution).
3. It tells you about what is near you (Information).

Quick List

- **Mandatory Signs** (round): Mandatory means compulsory. As the name suggests, these signs contain orders or instructions that every person on the road must follow.

  Not following these instructions can lead to the police charging a fine. These

This sign means 'One Way'

signs ensure the smooth flow of traffic and prevent crashes between vehicles.

- **Cautionary/Warning Signs** (triangle): These signs are useful for warning people about possible unsafe conditions on the road, especially for drivers.

  They warn against unsafe driving conditions, sharp turns or possible obstructions on the road.

This sign means that the 'Road Narrows on Both Sides Ahead'

- **Informatory Signs** (usually rectangle): These give information to road users. While they do not directly help in road safety, informative signs help people drive more safely and efficiently by telling them what is coming up on the road ahead.

  Information regarding nearby places and neighbourhoods, such as restaurants, is given through these signs. They also give driving directions to other parts of the city, or nearby cities.

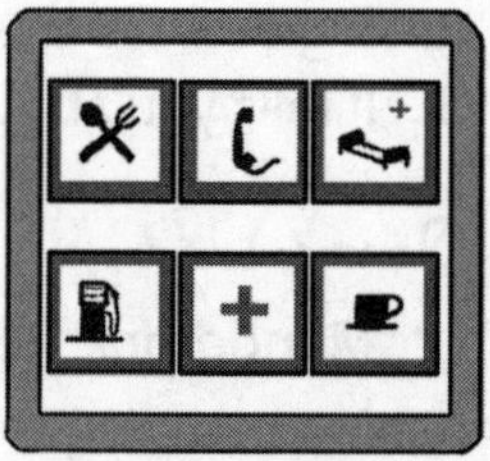

Guess what these signs are for!

SafeBook Says

"Apart from the three kinds of traffic signs, that is, circular, triangular and rectangular, there is also the stop sign. The shape of this sign is an octagon. This sign does not look like any of the above three categories. But the message is loud and clear. If you see a STOP sign, just STOP."

47 WHAT IF YOU ARE ALONE ON A PUBLIC BUS?

The horrific Nirbhaya Case rocked the nation a few years ago, when a woman was brutalized in a public bus in New Delhi and then left to die. It isn't possible to dismiss public transport travel entirely: it is cheaper, can save time on traffic-congested routes and is generally quite safe.

In any case, travelling at night or alone might raise a few safety concerns, and it is in these situations that you need to be extra careful.

Follow the tips below if you are alone on the bus or if the bus is not crowded.

DO

☑ Make a note of the number of the bus before boarding and share it with family and/or friends

☑ Use your smartphone smartly and share your live location with your friends and family for the duration of the journey.

☑ Get on a phone call if you feel anxious, and keep talking. This could discourage anyone from trying anything suspicious since the person at the other end of the line will immediately get to know.

☑ Keep your eyes and ears open – who is sitting or standing and where, what the driver or conductor is saying, what landmarks pass by…

☑ Take a note of the emergency exits and buttons inside the bus.

☑ Always carry a powerbank to keep your phone from running out of battery.

☑ Keep your belongings close to you.

☑ Ask the driver to stop at a bus stop and get on a different bus if you feel uncomfortable.

DON'T

☒ Simply hold the phone and pretend to talk. **Tip:** Please do speak to a real person. It will be embarrassing (and potentially dangerous) for you if somebody actually calls you while you are pretend-chatting!

- ☒ Give your name or address out loud on the phone.
- ☒ Get off in an isolated or poorly lit area.
- ☒ Take out your wallet or any expensive gadgets such as a laptop or a camera. Keep your bus money in a small, handy pouch.

SafeBook Says

"Nowadays, public buses come with a pre-installed panic button that can raise an alarm alerting the driver and people nearby. The driver is then required to stop the bus and intervene. Some buses are also equipped with CCTV cameras to monitor any suspicious activity. If your safety is under threat, use these facilities!"

Section Five

FOOD

48 FOOD-SHOPPING CHECKLIST

Don't diss it, guys! Choosing fruits and vegetables is an essential life skill. But how dangerous can a vegetable be, after all?

Quick Tips

- Select fruits and vegetables without spots or lesions. Discard those that appear to be infected by mould/fungus.
- Check for pests – wriggling worms are common in vegetables like cauliflower, ladies' finger, salad leaves and brinjal.
- Choose vegetables with nice bright colours. Discolouration is a no-no. Green vegetables with brown parts are clearly not fresh, so don't buy them.
- Good veggies are firm – neither hard nor squishy. Do NOT plunge your nail in to check.

That's a disgusting habit. You wouldn't want to find that the tomatoes you are buying have fingernail marks on them, would you? Carrots, beets, potatoes and onions should be hard with no cracks or soft spots.

- For fruits, it's important how they smell. If apples or oranges or plums or grapes are fragrant, they are ripe – go ahead and buy some. If a vegetable smells too sweet or sour, it's a NO.

DO

☑ Wash or scrub fruits and vegetables under running water, even if you do not plan to eat the peel. Germs on the peel or skin can get inside fruits and vegetables when you cut them. Raw fruits and vegetables contain harmful germs that can make you and your family sick, such as salmonella, E. coli and listeria. Discard the outer leaves of leafy vegetables such as lettuce and cabbage, so as to prevent pesticide residues from getting into your food.

☑ Keep pre-cut fruits and vegetables cold by choosing produce that is refrigerated or kept on ice.

☑ Separate fruits and vegetables from raw meat, poultry and seafood in your shopping cart and in your grocery bags. Wash your hands, kitchen utensils and food preparation surfaces, including chopping boards and countertops, before and after preparing fruits and vegetables.

☑ Refrigerate fruits and vegetables within 2 hours after you cut, peel or cook them (or 1 hour if the outside temperature is 32°C or warmer). Chill them at 0°C or colder in a clean container.

DON'T

☒ Wash fruits and vegetables with soap, detergent, dishwashing liquids or similar commercial produce washes.

☒ Do not use bleach solutions or other similar disinfecting products on food.

☒ Eat tomato leaves, apple seeds, cherry pits, peach or apricot stones, asparagus fruit, undercooked red kidney beans (rajma)... These are just a few very common and favourite foods or parts of foods that contain toxins. You could fall really ill if you consume the 'wrong' parts, particularly in large quantities. An apple seed here or a cherry pit there is not cause for concern, but just don't overdo it.

SafeBook Says

"A simple check: When buying fruits, take two similarly sized fruits and select the heavier one. Heavier produce is likelier to be juicier...and yummier!"

49 HOW TO BE SAFETY-SMART ABOUT EATING

At home, where does your food come from? The easy answer to that is: the kitchen. Now, think carefully before replying. What did it look like before it was ready to be served?

Our food comes in several different forms before it gets to your table. Look at the options:

1. Is it emptied out of a packet or box or bottle straight into a dish and eaten?
2. Is it in frozen form, thawed, then cooked, and served and eaten?
3. Is it raw to begin with, and is perhaps washed, chopped and/or cooked before being served?

If you answered option (3), bravo, that's the healthiest option. Let's look at options 1 and 2.

Packaged food: Very convenient, but it usually contains much more sugar and salt than is considered good for health. When in doubt, check the list of ingredients. Packaged food in India must carry the list of ingredients, but the law does not require the exact quantity of ingredients to

be printed. *Secret hack*: The ingredients are always listed in descending order of quantity. So, the first item listed is the item whose quantity makes up the bulk of the product. If you were to check a packet of potato chips, you'd see that the first item in the list is potatoes. Now, check out the list of ingredients on the wrapper of your favourite bar of chocolate. We can bet you will be surprised!

Frozen food: Freezing food products preserves them for longer. If this sounds obvious, here's the science. Low temperatures are not favourable for growth of microorganisms as the water in the food freezes. Moreover, enzyme activity and other chemical processes that cause food to spoil also slow down. Freezing also does not have much effect on the nutritional value of the food. So, food can be frozen, and eaten days, weeks or even months later as long as the freezing temperature stays constant. But note that frozen food, once thawed, should not be frozen again.

SafeBook Says

"Pasteurization (named after Louis Pasteur, who discovered it) is the process of treating foods (like milk and eggs) at mild temperatures to eliminate disease-causing microbes and extend the shelf life of the food."

50 HOW TO BE EVEN MORE SAFETY-SMART ABOUT EATING

Food goes right inside our bodies, and so do any harmful substances it may contain. What are the safety hazards of different foods?

While buying food products, choose fresh foods as much as possible. If you buy frozen foods, add them at the end to your trolley or basket so that you don't go around with them at room temperature for long. Make sure that the packaging is intact and that the item is sealed properly. We live in a hot country, so fresh foods should be refrigerated, and frozen foods should be placed in the freezer immediately.

- Dry flour (used in cake batter or bread dough) might contain bacteria such as E. coli. This contamination usually happens due to cattle droppings, and processes such as grinding and washing the wheat do not get rid of the bacteria. Cooking the flour properly kills the dangerous bacteria.

- Raw eggs may contain bacteria called salmonella, which can cause food poisoning and make you very ill. In fact, lightly boiled, runny or undercooked eggs are best avoided.
- Frozen foods, once thawed, are prone to spoilage thanks to the same bacteria, which can spread to other foods. So the food is best defrosted in its packaging. However, take out only what you are actually going to eat. Food that has been frozen and thawed should never be refrozen. A smart way to ensure this is to split food into portions before storing it in the freezer, so only small quantities are defrosted at a time. Frozen food can be defrosted slowly in the fridge. The low temperature slows the formation of bacteria although this takes a much longer time than defrosting it at room temperature.

DO

☑ Wash your hands with soap and running water after handling raw eggs, dough and mixes. Also clean the stove and other surfaces well.

☑ Follow cooking instructions (on packaged food, frozen or otherwise) properly so that you know the right cooking/baking time and temperature. Frozen food must be completely thawed before cooking unless the manufacturer's instructions say differently. Some frozen items can be deep-fried without thawing (French fries, potato smiles, nuggets and other snacks, where the instructions on the packets specifically mention not thawing).

☑ Heat the food thoroughly before eating when in doubt. Heating kills pathogens. But beware of repeated reheating. Food might lose all its nutrients.

DON'T

☒ Store raw flour and eggs with ready-to-eat foods.

☒ Eat play dough. We agree it is called dough, but it is just not edible.

SafeBook Says

"Bacteria grow most rapidly in temperatures ranging between 4°C and 60°C. Their numbers can actually double every 20 minutes. This range of temperatures is called the 'Danger Zone'."

51 FOOD-MED COMBOS

When a doctor prescribes medication of any kind, there are additional instructions on when to have the meds, before or after meals, and also, what one should or should not eat. This is because certain food items might not go well with the prescribed medicines. Here is the no-no list of food and meds combos, and the reasons for each, which are good to know about even if you may not be using any of these medicines.

Quick List

- ☐ **Dairy Products + Antibiotics:** Dairy products have calcium, which reacts with antibiotics to form a substance that cannot be absorbed by the body. Did you know this? No, you can't escape the milk entirely, but do leave a window of about three hours on either side of taking the antibiotic.
- ☐ **Green Vegetables + Anticoagulants:** Anticoagulants (such as aspirin) are used to

treat a range of conditions from a headache to a heart problem, by thinning the blood. Vitamin K, found in green vegetables, helps in blood clotting, which does the opposite job.

- ☐ **Coffee + Bronchodilators:** Bronchodilators relax and open the airway we use to breathe and are often used by people suffering from asthma and other breathing problems. Having caffeine-rich products such as coffee, tea and chocolate with these medicines can cause nervousness and rapid heartbeat.
- ☐ **Fermented/Pickled Food + Antidepressants:** Antidepressants known as MAOIs react with a compound called tyramine, which is present in cheese, yoghurt or pickles, to cause a sudden increase in blood pressure.
- ☐ **Grapefruit + Statins:** Statins are used for lowering cholesterol levels. Grapefruit blocks the enzymes that break down these medicines and can thus increase the quantity of statins entering the bloodstream, which could in turn lead to serious side effects.
- ☐ **Banana + ACE inhibitors:** These meds are used to lower blood pressure and relax the

blood vessels so that blood can flow more freely. They also increase the amount of potassium in the body, therefore, consuming potassium-rich foods such as banana, and oranges can be harmful as too much potassium causes irregular heartbeat and palpitations.

SafeBook Says

> **The common side effects of mixing certain food with medications include dizziness, nausea, fatigue, increased heart rate, and ineffectiveness of the medicine. *Always contact the doctor if the patient feels unwell after taking medicine.***

Section Six

THE INTERNET

52 WHAT DOES THE 'S' IN HTTPS:// MEAN?

Some websites use HTTPS instead of HTTP. Do you know why? Hyper-Text Transfer Protocol (HTTP) comprises the set of rules that determine how information is transferred over the Internet and almost all websites use it, but this does not have a security feature added into it. That's where the 'S' comes in. HTTPS stands for HTTP Secure.

If you look at the URL of a website and see 'HTTPS', it means the website is secured with an SSL (**S**ecure **S**ocket **L**ayer) certification and any data transmitted between your web browser and the server will be encrypted and secure. This ensures that online transactions or sensitive information is protected from scams and data thefts.

DO

☑ Check that the website uses *https* and has a green padlock displayed next to it in the URL bar.

- ☑ Check that the website has concrete contact information. All legitimate companies provide a valid phone number, email address and a physical address. If these details are missing, you could be on the wrong page.
- ☑ Check that a site has a privacy statement before you make any purchase from it.
- ☑ Check for the shipping and refund policy before making any transaction on an e-commerce website.

DON'T

- ☒ Use fake websites, which are badly designed with glaring spelling errors and have low-quality images and videos.
- ☒ Visit sites that offer unbelievable discounts.

SafeBook Says

> **Google boosts up websites using HTTPS rather than HTTP in its search rankings. Google ranks HTTPS sites and assigns a 'site quality' score along with their other factors such as page speed and mobile responsiveness. So, in a Google checklist, if a site is secure, it is likelier to pop up at the top of a search. Read up on search engine optimization or SEO for more in-depth information on this.**

53 WHAT'S A GOOD PASSWORD?

According to SplashData, a company that makes password managers, '123456' and 'password' occupied the two top spots on the 'Worst Passwords' list. A good password should be long, complex and as unique as possible.

A password should contain a mix of alphabets and numbers (what is called 'alphanumeric') and also have special characters so that it becomes difficult for password-cracking programs to guess your password. Using common phrases and terms makes it easy for hackers to crack your password. You can have fun creating secure passwords. Ideally your password should:

- **Have a minimum of 8 characters:** Make your password at least 8 characters long, but it can be 12 or 14 characters also, if you like.
- **Have numbers, symbols, capital letters, and lower-case Letters:** Use a combination of different types of characters to make your password harder to guess.

- **Not be a dictionary word or a combination of dictionary words:** Any obvious words or combination of words from the dictionary would make a poor password. For example, 'chocolate' would be a bad password, just as 'hotchocolate'.
- **Not contain obvious substitutions:** Avoid common replacements for characters, such as 'h0t; just because you've replaced an o with a 0, the password does not become stronger because it's very easy to crack that change.

The best way is to mix it up – for example, many of the above requirements are fulfilled by 'DarkChocolate&123' but it's a dictionary phrase where each word is capitalized properly. There's only one symbol, all the numbers are at the end, and they're in order too.

You can put any random password like 'cv7c54h4mm', but how would you ever remember it, unless you have a photographic memory! So, you have to be clever and think harder to come up with a memorable password. For instance, you might find it easier to remember a sentence like 'I want to have a hot chocolate at 6:30 in the morning'. Now turn that sentence into a password

SafeBook Says

> **"Hackers use a brute-force method called Dictionary Attack where they use the power of computers to guess passwords using words found in a dictionary."**

by using the first letter of each word, and a couple of contractions, so your password would become lwthhc@630am. This would be a much stronger password, and not difficult to recall either!

SafeBook Quiz

Do you know what to do to protect your device from hackers?

Put a tick for **DO** and a cross for **DON'T** in the square and see if you're right.

- ☐ Use common phrases, or words that are found in a dictionary.
- ☐ Use the same password for multiple services.
- ☐ Change your password every six months.
- ☐ Recycle passwords.
- ☐ Use a password manager to store and organize all your passwords.
- ☐ Enable two-factor authentication for your accounts wherein, after entering your password, a pin is sent to your phone to verify it.

54 HOW TO BE SMART ON SOCIAL MEDIA

Social media connects us to people across the globe. That's wonderful, isn't it? But, like all good things, it comes with a bunch of red flags. Can you be smarter on social media? You bet you can!

DO

- ☑ Choose strong passwords for your social media accounts. Make them all different. Use combinations of upper and lower case (capital and small) letters, numbers and special characters, and avoid names that can be easily guessed. The most hacked passwords include 123456, 1111, abcdef, QWERTY and suchlike.
- ☑ Check your privacy and location settings. All social media companies allow you to choose who can see your information. Keep this setting to 'friends only' instead of 'public'.
- ☑ Remember, it's a good idea to check with mutual friends before accepting any friend request from someone you dont know well.

- ☑ Keep in mind that an Internet troll is someone who bullies or harasses you on social media. Just do not respond to them. Just DON'T! We cannot say this strongly enough. Report and block their profiles so that they can no longer interact with you.
- ☑ Speak to your elders (parents and teachers) and let them know if you feel threatened or the bullying continues. They will help you out in such situations by reporting the troll to the police or other relevant authorities.

DON'T

- ☒ Ever share your personal address, phone number or location in your posts.
- ☒ Accept friend requests from people you don't know or haven't met personally. Do not chat with them online and never share your personal pictures.

☒ Let your friends post any picture or information about you online without your permission.

SafeBook Says

> **According to the Children's Online Privacy Protection Act (COPPA), a person must be at least 13 years of age to use the services of most social media sites and create his/her account. This is to protect American kids. There are no specific Indian laws to protect Indian children on international social media sites, but hey, laws and rules exist for a reason. Don't break them!**

55 PHISHING, PHARMING AND OTHER KINDS OF 'PHRAUD'

Sorry to burst the bubble, but there is no African billionaire leaving you their fortune. Neither have you won the lottery nor a top-end mobile phone, nor a treasure chest full of gold. The minute you click on that tempting link or reply to that mail (bait), your data and/or money are at risk.

The Internet bait lures the poor fish (that's you, my friend!) and that's where the word phishing comes from. If you reply, your identity, location and other personal information can be 'read' by the phisher. Worse, if you share bank or credit card details (of your parents, for instance), you can lose money faster than a mouse-click!

Pharming, on the other hand, is known as 'phishing without a lure' where the attacker installs a malicious (nasty, mean, bad) code on your computer that whisks you off to fraudulent websites instead of legitimate ones. Again, your personal information can be misused.

Phishing targets one person while pharming can attack multiple users at once.

Take a look at these other cyber-security terms you should know about:

Quick List

Potential phishers or pharmers target you in a variety of ways for a number of reasons. This quick list has some of the ways in which you can get hit, along with the probable intention of the miscreant.

- **Identity fraud:** The attacker steals the identity of a user and uses it to make financial transactions. The victim may end up losing a LOT of money.

- **Keylogger:** A malicious code starts recording the key strokes on the victim's computer to obtain sensitive information such as passwords and other details for future abuse.
- **Malware:** this is software that causes harm to the user. 'Mal' is short for malicious or malevolent, both of which boil down to 'bad'.
- **Ransomware:** A malware that encrypts data (jams, freezes, makes it unreadable) on the victim's computer, so it cannot be used. This is followed by demands for money in exchange for the key to decode the data. Nasty, we agree.
- **Spam:** These are unwanted e-mails and messages that are sent out in large numbers to multiple users. Most spam consists of advertisements, but sometimes there could be malicious hyperlinks or attachments that are best left unopened.
- **Spyware:** This is a malware that literally spies on the user and monitors user activities. The data is then sent to a third party. Attackers learn a lot about the user and can then cause further harm.
- **Virus:** This is the best-known term. A virus is a malware that often attaches itself to a host computer and starts infecting files on that system (like a virus in a human body!). Viruses can destroy and corrupt data or really slow down the system. A virus can be transferred

from computer to computer when connected on the same network or via USB/pen drives. Viruses are of different types – they could corrupt certain kinds of software or files, or the entire hard drive.

The above can make your life miserable as well as expose you to risks/danger. Here are some general dos and don'ts to keep your devices – and you – safe.

DO

☑ Keep your device software updated.

☑ Install an updated antivirus package on your device.

☑ Use two-factor authentication* (*see next page*) wherever possible.

☑ Stay alert when you give up personal information in public places.

☑ Set strong passwords on your devices.

☑ Keep your data backed up.

DON'T

☒ Open links sent by strangers.

☒ Save important files or folders on your desktop.

☒ Shop on unknown shopping portals; check their antecedents first.

☒ Type PIN or passwords in public view.

☒ Open flash drives or USB devices without running a security check.

Quick Check

* Two-factor authentication is an extra layer of security when you want access to a website, device or app. It usually has two steps, which is why it is also called two-step authentication. The steps could be a combination of:
  - **Knowledge** (what you know): password, PIN, security question, etc.
  - **Possession** (what you have): card, key, etc.
  - **Inherence** (what you are): fingerprint, iris or face unlock, voice, etc.
  - **Location** (where you are): GPS locator.

SafeBook Says

> **Proper websites never ask you to change passwords or interfere with your login information by sending emails with links. If you ever see a mail asking for information related to your account, and they want your password or any OTP in reply, sit tight. Send nothing. The only time you should reset your password is if you ask for it yourself.**

56 HOW TO MAKE YOUR WI-FI CONNECTION MORE SECURE

Once upon a time, in the twentieth century, you could access the Internet on your computer via something called an ethernet cable – one device only. But now, there's Wi-Fi! Multiple devices like smartphones, tablets, smart home devices – even light bulbs – can be connected on the same Wi-Fi to the Internet.

The Wi-Fi router is a super-valuable device at home. The router uses radio frequencies to send signals between devices. Within that range, a certain number of devices can be used. Your router – your gateway to the Internet – is prone to attack by cybercriminals who can hack your connection and get access to all the devices connected via Wi-Fi. The good news is that a secure connection can help.

Quick Tips

- Change the default name (SSID) of your Wi-Fi network to something personalized.

Most router manufacturers use a set default name. Just change this name, so hackers would find it hard to guess which company's router you have.

- Choose a strong and random password that cannot be guessed easily. Do not use the default password that comes with the router.
- Use a strong encryption standard to secure your wireless network, like WPA (short for Wi-Fi Protected Access) or WPA2. The latter is more secure than the former.
- Like computer software, hardware can also have its own firewall. Buy a Wi-Fi router with an in-built firewall.
- Update all your devices – which means the router too – with the latest software updates.
- Change your network admin username and the password regularly (you will find it on the Wi-Fi router when you set up your Wi-Fi).

SafeBook Says

> Do you know what a VPN is? A VPN, or a 'virtual private network', creates a separate private network in your main Wi-Fi network. VPN software then encrypts all the data that is transferred over the private network. This is great because no one else can access your data!

57 HOW TO LOCK YOUR SMARTPHONE, SMARTLY

Our smartphones contain a crazy amount of information about us: our social media accounts, messenger apps, list of contacts, emails, photos, videos and more. Earning members even have apps for financial transactions, like banking apps and credit card details. So it's absolutely essential to keep the phone safe from prying eyes.

There are lots of ways to lock our phones: PIN, Password, Pattern, Fingerprint, or Face Unlock, depending on the model. How efficient are these locking systems? Read on…

Quick List

- **PIN:** The PIN (**P**ersonal **I**dentification **N**umber) has been in use now for ages, even before smartphones. The four-digit PIN is the most common, but you can keep longer PINs – like 6-digit PINs – if you wish. The easier or shorter the PIN, the easier it is to unlock, and not just by the phone owner either… Got it?

- **Password:** The password option is more secure than a PIN, as it allows you to use a combination of letters of the alphabet, numbers and special characters. This option is quite secure, but of course typing a complicated password (and remembering it!) means it takes longer to unlock your phone.
- **Pattern:** Android phones popularized the Pattern lock which lets you create a pattern by connecting dots to unlock your phones. Pattern locks are much faster than typing a PIN or a password. However, people nearby can easily guess the pattern if they observe your finger movements – and recreate the pattern.
- **Fingerprint:** This is fast, secure and easy to do because you don't have to remember anything. Your fingerprint is unique, so only you can unlock the phone. Two

SafeBook Says

> **Be smarter than your smartphone. Choose a PIN that is relevant to you, one that you will remember. Don't pick sitters like 1234 or 123456 (just anyone will be able to open your phone with those) and even very easily guessed ones, such as your birthdate or birth year.**

things to think of: don't operate your phone while eating greasy or messy food, and make sure nobody presses your unlocking finger on your phone as you sleep :).

- **Face Unlock:** These are very cool locks. But the unlock speed depends on (a) the quality of your phone; (b) its front-facing camera; and (c) lighting, so a fingerprint unlock is usually quicker. Also, Face Unlocks can sometimes be fooled by a picture of the phone's owner!

58 THE DARK SIDE OF SOCIAL MEDIA

These days, social media is a mirror of our lives! What we do daily – what we ate for breakfast, whom we met, what we are wearing, what we read and what we think, our good and bad hair days – everything is now fodder for a post, a reel, a story or a tweet. What's dangerous about that?

Documenting our lives is not a bad thing per se. A whole new generation has learnt to showcase events using text, images, audio and video, and read about and react to world happenings on social media. So what about all this makes it a suitable topic in a book on safety? The trouble is that, sometimes, you can get confused about what is real and what is not.

In particular, here are some red flags that you should be aware of:

☒ **Don't share information**. When you share your birthdate, the names of your pets, or your favourite sports teams, books, authors or musicians, you are also giving potential identity thieves a peek into your passwords. And don't ever share real-time pictures of your vacations. You don't want people to know that your home is empty. Think about it…

☒ **Private ≠ safe**. Your own settings may be private, but your friends and followers might not have such settings. Privacy means control, and each time you share a picture or video, post a comment or even just an emoji, you are transferring that control to all those with whom you have shared that thought, moment, event, whatever. And once it's posted, there is **no delete button**. EVER. It is always there on the Internet. So before you post something you might regret later, here are two questions you might want to ask:

- ☐ Is this something I would say or do face-to-face?
- ☐ Would I be OK with this photo or meme or text being posted in the school corridors?

Hmmm, we thought so, too.

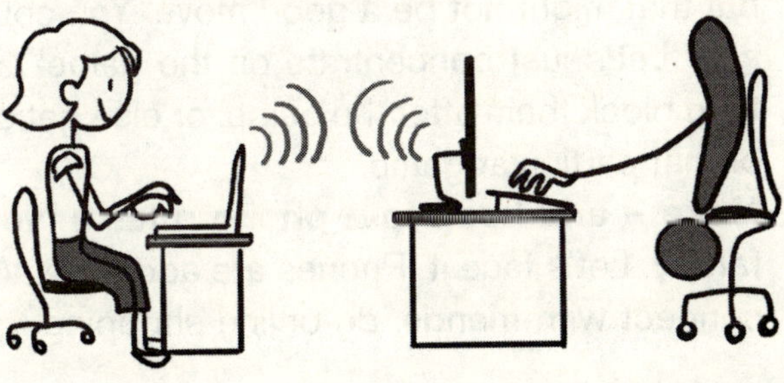

☒ **Don't get on social media too young**. Tweens, (<13-years-olds), we're talking to you. There's a reason why some movies are not for kids, why kids cannot get a driver's licence and why you cannot vote. While you may 'get away' with lying about your age on a social media platform, we urge you to think twice. Why? Because there are trolls, stalkers, predators and nasty people out there, disguised as 'friends' or 'followers', and content that is genuinely unsuitable for children. You are going to spend your entire lives as adults. Enjoy your time minus social media is what we'd say. It's a lot of fun to NOT be on a screen, scrolling mindlessly.

☑ **Watch out for predators**. When you are online, chatting, gaming or going through post comments, if, say, a friend of a friend tries to chat you up, ask you questions you are not comfortable with or makes uncomfortable comments about you, inform a parent or older sibling immediately. It means this person is not safe. You could block a player while gaming, but that might not be a good move. You could say, 'Let's just concentrate on the game' and then block them after the game, or else get out of that particular game.

☑ **Make – and keep to – phone rules in your family**. Let's face it. Phones are addictive. We connect with friends, do online shopping, get entertained and even attend online school if required, on our phones. But it is a good idea to detox from the phone at pre-defined times in the day: meal times, an hour for exercising or sport, an hour before sleeping, and so on. Also, do use number-tracing apps like Truecaller so that you can (a) identify unwanted callers and then block them (b) identify spam callers and (c) report calls that are potentially dangerous, such as unidentifiable numbers or unknown numbers from abroad, to your parents or even the police.

☑ **Beware of the marketing**. All free social media platforms make money through advertising. As a user, you are also one of their 'products': your profile, location, interests, posts, the sites you visit, share or comment on...every single online activity is tracked and used for targeted ads. If you like a singer or band or celebrity or cartoon character and share some posts about them, merchandise companies might show you branded T-shirts or bags or all kinds of merchandise. But some of the targeted marketing is fake or malicious.* If you are ever invited by a sponsored site to share personal or financial details, stop right there and consult a trusted adult.

* *Want to know more? See 'Phishing, Pharming and Other Kinds of 'Phraud'.*

- **Don't create finsta and rinsta (fake and real instagram) accounts.** Like, one for the family and one for followers that your parents might not approve of. The same for other social media platforms. It's untidy, complicated and will mess up your life. Work out boundaries with your parents.*

SAFEBOOK SAYS

> **Social media is here to stay, and there's no escape. But like the 'offline' world, the Internet is also a public place, and the rules are for everyone. Don't be a bully, don't be abusive and don't engage with faceless, nameless people who hide behind a 'profile'. Be polite, be decent, be kind, and be yourself. And be cautious. The real you has no filters.**

***Note to parents:** Please never ever scold or shame your child online, for everyone to see.*

59 HOW TO MANAGE SCREEN TIME

Raise your hand if you have a hard time falling asleep at night! Raise your hand again if the last thing you do before sleeping is to check your phone or tablet or watch TV. Here's the thing: it's not your fault if you cannot sleep. The reason is technology.

Modern gadgets with LED screens all have one thing in common: blue light. You might have noticed that the screen gives off a bluish tinge. And what's the problem with that? Well, it reduces or even stops the production of melatonin, the sleep-inducing hormone. And so, your eyes simply do not shut at all!

Our bodies need sleep to function optimally. Seven to eight hours of sleep truly help us rejuvenate and function better during our working day.

So you can do one of two things:

1. The best thing is to NOT stare into a screen before sleeping. So, no mindless scrolling on social media platforms, viewing of shows or

videos, or chit-chatting with friends on chat/ DM. Read a book or even an e-reader with no backlight, listen to soothing music or talk with family members until you nod off.

2. Be on a screen – if you MUST – but change the settings to orange or some other warm light. Else you could wear warm tinted goggles, with orange or brown lenses. Apple and Android devices and even desktops have apps that help you change screen light.

SafeBook Says

"Studies everywhere advise us against staring at a screen for hours and hours. It literally robs us of our sleep. Use the night light feature or install night shift on your devices and enjoy a good night's sleep!"

Section Seven

NATURAL DISASTERS

60 WHAT IS THE 30/30 RULE FOR THUNDERSTORMS?

Have you noticed that in all scary films the frightening things always happen during a thunderstorm? There are blinding flashes of lightning, deafening claps of thunder and pelting rain. But the heroes and heroines have clearly never heard of the slogan: *When thunder roars, go indoors!*

Thunderstorms can be frightening; the rumbles are not dangerous by themselves but are always accompanied by their deadly companion – lightning. A bolt of lightning can contain around one billion volts of energy (the entire city of New York can be powered for 26 minutes in that much!). According to a study by the National Crime Records Bureau, an average of 2,360 people have died in India every year due to lightning since 2001, so it's better to be safe than sorry.

The 30/30 rule helps in safeguarding yourself against lightning strikes. Remember that light travels faster than sound, so you'll always see lightning before you hear the thunderclap. Start counting when you see lightning until you hear the thunder. If you don't make it to 30, seek shelter immediately. If you didn't see the lightning, hearing a thunderclap is a good enough signal to head indoors.

The other 30 means that you should stay in that shelter for at least 30 minutes after you have heard the last roar of thunder, as the storm might not be over. Here are our quick tips to help you if find yourself stuck in a thunderstorm either indoors or outdoors:

REMEMBER! Never take shelter under a tree. Lightning has a greater chance of striking taller objects like buildings and trees. If the topmost point of the tree gets struck by lightning, it can travel all the way to the ground and jump on you.

DO

If you are indoors:

☑ Avoid water, i.e., taking a shower, doing the dishes, washing your hands, doing the laundry, because water can conduct electricity.

SafeBook Says

“There was a 22.6 per cent increase in lightning in India in 2020 compared to 2019, according to the '2020 India Lightning Report' released by Earth Networks. Karnataka and Maharashtra were among the top 10 states with the highest lightning pulse.”

☑ Switch off heavy electronic equipment to avoid any damage to them.
☑ Stay away from glass panes and windows as the high winds can cause them to shatter.
☑ Stop using a landline telephone as lightning may strike the phone lines and electric charges can be transmitted.

If you are outdoors:
☑ Take shelter immediately in an enclosed structure. If you can't find one, squat with your head cushioned in your folded arms resting on your knees.

☑ Get off bicycles or motorcycles. Stay inside a closed car that can shield you from electric discharges.
☑ Get out of a large group; spread out.
☑ Avoid being in a waterbody – head to terra firma (solid ground) immediately.

61 FLOOD ALERT!

A flood occurs when rainwater, rivers, seas or other waterbodies overflow onto land and cover it with water. Floods are an annual natural disaster due to rain in our country. Now the incidence of floods is increasing all over the world due to global warming and climate change: the polar ice caps are melting, and water levels in the oceans are rising.

Thanks to science, we know the courses of rivers. Yet, a combination of reduced forest cover, poor town planning and unchecked construction have actually ignored the floodplains of rivers and covered them with roads and buildings. Under such circumstances, floods are inevitable. Once a flood occurs, disease and death follow. So it's a good idea to be prepared if you know that your city or neighbourhood is likely to get flooded.

DO

- ☑ Stock food, especially food items that won't perish easily, like potatoes and onions, cereals, pulses and packaged foods.
- ☑ If you live in a low-lying area or are on the ground floor, move delicate and expensive items and food items off the floor.
- ☑ Unplug electrical items and move them to safer spots in the house. If you can close sockets, do so, to prevent the possibility and incidence of electric shock or short circuits.
- ☑ If you can move with family to an upper floor or safer zone temporarily, do so.
- ☑ Keep over-the-counter (OTC) medicines for stomach upsets and electrolyte solutions.
- ☑ Store up on drinking water. Drink only safe water. During a flood, we are surrounded by water, but none of it can be consumed!
- ☑ Keep yourself healthy. You cannot get to a doctor easily if you fall ill.
- ☑ If you are outdoors and caught in floodwaters, stay away from vehicles. If you are a passenger in a vehicle, please tell the driver not to drive fast. It might look like fun to make a tremendous splash, but apart from being an insensitive thing to do, it is also unsafe: water will enter your own vehicle and stall it.

- ☑ Put sandbags in the toilet bowl and cover all drain holes to prevent sewage backflow. The backflow is likely to occur because the flooding causes a swell in the stormwater and sewer drains, and the increased pressure makes that extra water rush into low-lying areas, like basements, ground-floor toilets and so on. Do note that this is an emergency measure. The long-term solution to preventing sewage backflow is to install a backflow valve in the main sewer line, but that would involve municipal authorities and sewage experts.
- ☑ When leaving the house, turn off the power and gas connections.
- ☑ Take the emergency kit* with you.
- ☑ After the flood, throw away things like rugs that cannot be disinfected. Wash floors and walls with water and soap/disinfectant.

In case of a flood, go up to the roof or any higher ground

* *Great, but what should you put inside this? See 'What to Pack in an Emergency Kit?"*

DON'T

- ☒ Step out of home without reason. If your area is flooded and you are stuck at home, there's very little you can do until the water ebbs away.
- ☒ Floodwaters can have dangerous currents, and you can drown. If stagnant, the waters attract insects, snakes and other creepy-crawlies. Plus floodwaters are mucky and garbage-ridden. You do not want to catch some dreaded disease, so stay indoors!
- ☒ Go near water sewage lines, gutters, electrical lines and poles.
- ☒ Use food and water that has been through the floodwater. Throw it away.
- ☒ Use electrical devices and gadgets that are or have been moist or wet – use them only after getting them checked.
- ☒ Enter deep, unknown waters; use a stick to check water depth

SafeBook Says

"Plant more trees, study about climate change and global warming, and do your bit for the planet. Our Earth will survive even if it gets covered in water, but we human beings will not."

62 WHAT TO DO WHEN THE GROUND IS MOVING?

Earthquakes occur due to the movement of large areas, called tectonic plates, beneath the earth's surface. As the plates move towards each other, their edges snag and start gnashing against each other, building up pressure. When the pressure is severe enough, it is released as energy that literally rocks the earth's surface and causes an earthquake. Earthquakes can strike anywhere and without any warning.

Large office and residential buildings usually have an evacuation plan in place for earthquakes. Many schools also have regular earthquake drills, so you may already know what to do. But if you don't, here are the important points to keep in mind.

First of all, don't panic. Grab your emergency kit quickly if there is enough time.

DO

- ☑ Stay indoors, if you are indoors.
- ☑ DROP, COVER AND HOLD ON. Drop to the ground, get under a table and stay there until the shaking stops.

- ☑ Stay away from windows and pieces of heavy furniture or appliances that could fall on you.
- ☑ If you are outdoors, get away from buildings, trees and power lines or anything that can fall on you.
- ☑ If you're in a car, slow down and drive to a safe place – an open area is ideal. Stay in the car until the shaking stops.
- ☑ If you are in a hilly terrain, watch out for landslides and falling rocks that may occur even after the shaking stops.
- ☑ Turn off the gas by turning off the main entry valve in the pipe (or cylinder) and the electricity, by turning off the main power switch of the house. Gas pipes and wiring running underground can leak when the ground itself is wobbly, potentially causing more damage.

DON'T

- ☒ Stay inside the kitchen.
- ☒ Go outside while the building is shaking as debris could fall on you.

SafeBook Quiz

What scale is used to measure the intensity of an earthquake? Earthquakes of a greater magnitude than 6 on this scale can cause a lot of damage near the epicentre (that's where the earthquake starts from).

63 WHAT ALL TO PACK IN AN EMERGENCY KIT?

Prepare and prevent, goes an old saying. Dashing at the last minute to get important things together in a time of potential danger not only makes it stressful for you, but it's also likely that you will forget things or end up panicking. Keep an emergency backpack or other easily portable bag ready at all times.

Once you have your bag packed, do keep checking from time to time, for instance, for expiry dates on foodstuff, medicines and batteries, say, every six months. Keep the bag in a place from where it's easy to pick it up in a rush. On the next page is a list of what you need to have in your emergency kit (of course, you can chop and change as you like according to your own individual situation and needs).

What to put in your emergency/disaster kit

Essentials

Non-perishable packaged foods

Water

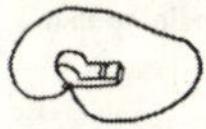
Whistle

Area map and compass

Can opener

Torch, transistor with batteries

First-aid kit

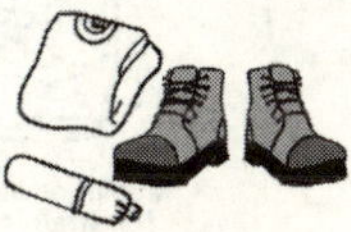
Clothes, rainwear, sturdy shoes

Wrench or plier

Other Necessary Items

Medicines, glasses

Aluminium foil

Paper and pencil/pen

Candles and matches

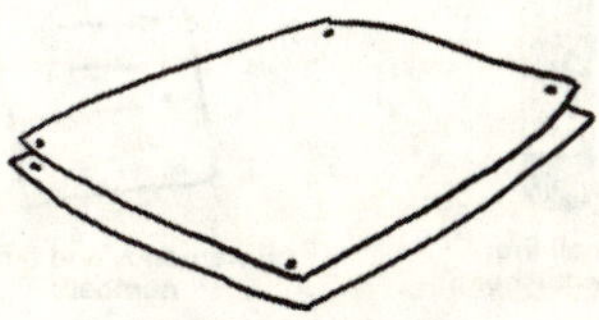
Tarpaulin 8 x 10 feet

Thick sheet/sleeping bag/blanket

Rope

Water purification kit or tablets for water

Knife and razor blades

Mini toolkit

Plastic utensils and cups

Plastic Ziploc bags

Muslin or other cloth for straining water

A basic mobile with charger

Supplies and food for babies and the elderly

Waterproof box or file case with important documents such as IDs

Paper towels

Small fire extinguisher

Emergency and family numbers

Set of extra keys for the house, vehicle and others

Money

Toiletries

Games, books and other activities

Section Eight

THE OUTDOORS

64 WHAT TO REMEMBER WHEN GOING SWIMMING

Swimming can be the best thing in summer (except for mangoes and ice cream, perhaps!). But water is not a natural habitat for humans – I mean, we know that. So, it's best to follow safety rules when in the water.

A tragic statistic is that drowning is one of the major causes of injuries and death among kids all over the world. When water gets in the lungs, oxygen flow is blocked, and in a few minutes, the body loses consciousness and the person, sadly, dies.

Here's what to keep in mind while swimming:

DO

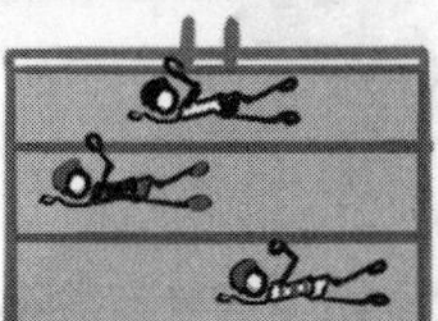

- ☑ Make sure you always swim under adult supervision. Never go swimming alone.
- ☑ Always obey pool rules. If the pool is closed, it means the lifeguard is off duty. So don't get into the pool.

☑ Remember, flotation toys and devices help you to learn swimming, but they cannot save your life, especially in a natural water body. So those cute little arm guards and rings might help you float, but they are useless against a strong current.

☑ Stay in the shallows if you are learning to swim. It's common sense! At all times, stay in designated safe areas.

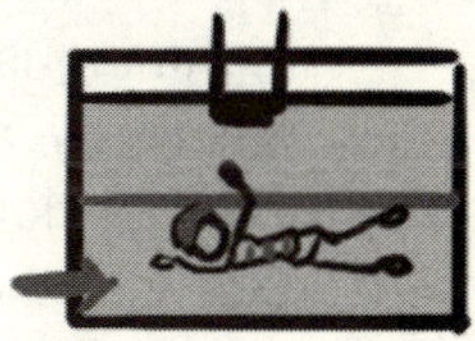

☑ Wear something to protect your feet if you are swimming in a lake or a pond. The lake or pond bed could be rocky. Lakes and ponds are very different from pools – they may be full of entangling weeds too.

☑ Keep in mind that swim caps and eyewear are good for hygiene – both yours and that of your co-swimmers.

☑ Drink plenty of water and fluids when swimming. Funnily, being in water can dehydrate you! (We especially refer to salt water, or a heated pool.)

DON'T

☒ Run in the pool area or play around in the water. One slip or silly move and you could literally be in deep water!

- ☒ Swim in moving water.
- ☒ Chew gum or eat while you swim. It's a choking hazard.
- ☒ Swim in the dark. Stop swimming if you hear a storm and get out of the water immediately. Lightning is millions of volts of electricity, and electricity and water make for a dangerous combination.
- ☒ Get into the water if you feel the water is too hot or too cold. Always first check to see if the water's temperature is comfortable for you to swim in.
- ☒ Walk near a pool/waterbody unnecessarily.

SafeBook Says

"Did you know that lifeguards have a 10/20 protection rule? If a lifeguard spots someone in trouble, s/he needs to respond in 10 seconds and reach the person in 20 seconds."

65 GPS HAS LOST SIGNAL... HIT REFRESH?

GPS stands for Global Positioning System. Using space satellites, a GPS phone app like Google Maps can help us navigate roads, brave traffic and correctly estimate how much time we will take to reach somewhere. But what if it's not working?

Now, let's run a set of what ifs. What if the phone battery runs out? What if GPS signal is lost? What if you are lost in a low-network coverage area, like the woods? How would you navigate?

Before we share our bag of tricks, some free advice: always inform your elders where you are going and whether you are going alone or with a group of people. It's also a good idea to carry a paper map of the place (say, on camping trips) or an offline version of the map on your smartphone.

Quick Tips

- Carry a compass (a real one, not an app).

- If you get lost during the day (without a compass), use the sun. It's easy. The sun rises in the east and sets in the west, correct? Learn to read which way you are facing from that piece of knowledge. Then use the map to find your way out.
- At night, the stars will guide you. The easiest way to get a sense of direction is spotting the North Star, Polaris, which always points north. You can find the position of Polaris from the Big Dipper constellation.

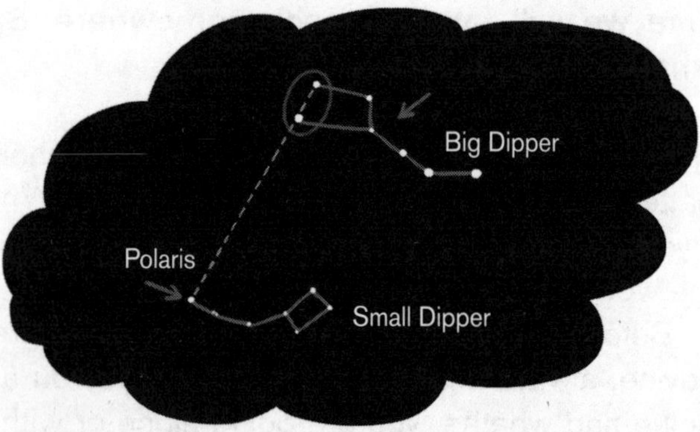

- If you get lost in the city, it is easier. There are signs, hoardings and buildings – look at them and read. The first step to take is to identify where you are.
- Next, start moving by keeping track of landmarks so that you don't end up moving in circles. In the fairy tale, Hansel dropped

smooth white stones, with which to find his way back out of the woods – but, oops, you cannot do that in town!

- Try locating a place of worship, like a temple, church or mosque. They can be easily found and can give you a sense of direction. For example, mosques in India always face west, towards Mecca, with entry from the east.

SafeBook Says

"The Big Dipper has an Indian name too. It is called Saptarishi, or the seven sages!"

66 SAFETY IN THE GREAT OUTDOORS

Hiking, trekking, and camping are great opportunities to connect with nature. Apart from the adventure, they are a super way to bond with your friends and family, and leave you with memories for a lifetime. But nature is unpredictable, and it's good to be ready for the unexpected.

Ample planning and advance preparation are key. Want to be trek-safe and trek-smart? Read on.

Quick Tips

Note these:

- Prepare the itinerary (well in advance).

- Share it with all your co-travellers.
- Prepare an emergency plan in case someone goes missing.
- Everyone should carry a cell phone and a personal locating beacon or a whistle.
- Everyone must be aware of helpline and emergency numbers.

Pack these clothes:

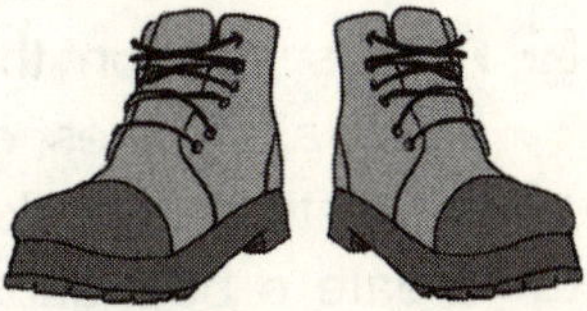

- Waterproof jacket (especially if you go trekking in hilly places – it can get cold really quickly).
- Bright-coloured clothes such as those in neon yellow or green. They will help keep your body cool and increase your chances of being spotted if lost.
- Long pants (they will protect you from brambles, thorns, burrs and creepy-crawlies).
- Proper hiking boots and socks.

Carry these in your first-aid kit:

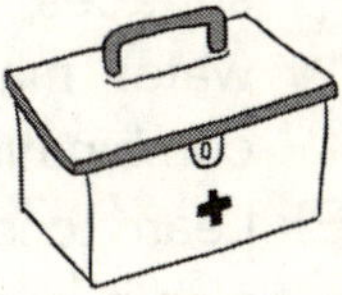

- Band-aid strips
- Medical tape
- Antiseptic ointment
- Emergency medication for fever, allergies and vomiting

Keep these handy:

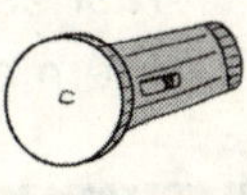

- Tents and sleeping bags
- High-protein snacks
- Water bottle
- Torch
- Paper map
- Whistle
- Strong rope
- Garbage bags

DO

- ☑ Always stay on the trail and stay with your group at all times, even when you need to visit the restroom or take a shower.
- ☑ Create a boundary around your campsite by attaching strings to trees and *stay within that boundary, like, ALWAYS*. Wandering off alone or playing games such as hide-and-seek is a bad idea.
- ☑ Waterbodies are beautiful but dangerous. Do not step into running water. Do not climb around waterfalls. Loose rocks, slippery surfaces and fast-flowing water make for a deadly combination.
- ☑ Learn to identify dangerous plants, such as poison oak/ivy. Keep washing your hands frequently to avoid rashes if you brush against them accidentally.

DON'T

- ☒ Eat anything that you find in the woods, like berries, nuts or mushrooms.

☒ Keep food in the tent. Animals have a very keen sense of smell and could barge into the tent for a snack.

☒ Leave ANY traces of your trek – dispose of your trash and do not ever leave anything that is not biodegradable. Remember that there is no garbage disposal in nature, and you don't want to be responsible for poisoning or killing curious animals who might pop your garbage into their mouths. Their safety is also in your hands.

SafeBook Says

> **Make some noise when you're walking through the woods to warn nearby animals to stay away. If you do come across a wild animal, back away slowly and give them their space. Do not run or turn your back to the animal. You could carry pepper-spray, but please *learn how to use it first and never, ever use it on an animal unless there is grave danger.***

67 HOW TO TAKE A SMART SELFIE

The most shared personal pictures on social media are selfies. We do agree that you look your best in a selfie, but make sure it's a safe and not sorry one!

Taking your own picture in your room is one thing, and taking daring selfies at cliff precipices, waterfalls, rail tracks and other dangerous but thrilling venues is another – an unnecessary weird-flex and a completely dumb idea.

DO

☑ Get a firm foothold wherever you are standing for a selfie.

☑ Be aware of your surroundings.

DON'T

☒ Take a selfie while crossing the street, driving, biking or using other moving equipment.

☒ Stand on the edge of a roof, cliff or ledge.

☒ Take a selfie close to waterbodies. Gushing water has ended up drowning people in groups taking selfies. Do not underestimate the force of water.

☒ Take a selfie on the go, i.e., while walking or on a cycle, or on the road.

Dangerous!

Be smarter and safer

☒ Try taking a selfie too close to wildlife. Animals are generally in the mood for food rather than pictures.

- ☒ Force animals to pose. This also goes for strangers' pets.
- ☒ Pose on mountain or clifftops, high-rise buildings, roofs or bridges. The most selfie deaths have been of people falling from heights. Don't lean out too far.
- ☒ Stand on railway tracks or trains.
- ☒ Be careful of electrical wiring and fast-moving vehicles.
- ☒ Take selfies with explosives or dangerous objects nearby.
- ☒ Ignore safety enclosures and posted rules about safe areas and taking photographs.

SafeBook Says

> **India holds the dubious distinction of having more selfie deaths than any other country in the world, more than 200 in this decade. As recently as July 2021, 11 people died of a lightning strike. Why? Because some of them were taking selfies. During a storm. On top of a tower. Unnecessary and fatal. Selfies that end up killing the self-photographer are called killfies, and are *all avoidable*.**

68 HOW TO PUT OUT A CAMPFIRE

If you have been on a camping trip, or even only seen it on screen, you would know that no camping trip is complete without a campfire around which people sit and sing or share spooky stories and make lasting memories. A warm fire on a cold winter evening or during a Lohri celebration is of the same kind.

Yes, campfires are fun for sure, but as soon as that last story or song is over and it's time to go into your tents for the night, it is extremely important to make sure that you have put out the fire completely. These campfires, if not extinguished properly, can quickly turn into a wildfire and lead to large-scale devastation, especially if there are forests nearby, endangering its flora and fauna as well as the people who live close to the area.

DO

☑ Pour dirt over the embers of the fire and stir it with a stick until the fire is extinguished.

- ☑ Let the fire burn itself out fully, i.e., until all the wood/coal has been completely reduced to ash. This is the best option, and a little bit of planning ahead makes sure that you don't add too much fuel to your fire.
- ☑ Use a shovel or a stick to spread the remaining wood or coal so that they are not touching each other. This helps to extinguish the fire quickly.

☑ Sprinkle water on the fire and the embers and keep sprinkling until you stop hearing the hissing sound. If you do not have water, you can also use dirt or sand to smother the fire.

☑ Lower your hand above the ash, if you can still feel the heat radiating, repeat the above steps.

☑ A final check, always, to ensure that there are no embers or sparks left before you leave.

Remember!

DO NOT simply bury the fire with the dirt — a buried fire can smoulder and then re-ignite.

SafeBook Says

"Don't ever add materials like tyres, plastic, cloth or glass to a bonfire. They will release horrible gases and fumes as they burn and melt, and your lungs will breathe in all the toxins."

Section Nine

PERSONAL

69 HOME ALONE?

Lucky you! If you have been left alone at home, it's because your parents feel that you are old enough to stay home and act responsibly. Here are a few steps to ensure you stay safe and know what to do in case of an emergency.

(Oh, and by the way, the *Home Alone* series of films is *not* realistic or something to wish for; but you know that, don't you?)

Here's what to keep in mind while you are alone at home:

DO

☑ Follow the rules that your parents set, like who can be allowed to enter the house, what to say if the phone rings, and so on.

☑ Lock all the doors and windows from the inside to prevent anyone from breaking in.

☑ Keep emergency numbers handy – it is best to memorize them. These numbers include 100 for Police, 101 for Fire Brigade and 102 for Ambulance, along with the contact numbers of your parents and neighbours.

☑ Be attentive at all times. Take a round of the house once in a while to ensure that the doors and windows are locked properly and there are no other warning signs such as smoke or fire. Sitting inside a room with the music blaring or headphones on is not a great idea.

☑ Keep the lights switched on in different rooms after dark, so that an outsider would think that more than one person is at home.

DON'T

☒ Open the door to strangers. If there's a package, let the delivery agent leave it on the doorstep (it's easier nowadays, post-COVID). Do not tell the messenger that you are alone.

☒ Post about being home alone on social media.

☒ Leave the house unless you have been asked to; always check with your parents before stepping out.

☒ Play with knives, scissors, matchboxes and anything that could hurt you. Stay away from cleaning liquids and medicines.

SafeBook Says

> **Practise an emergency plan with your parents so that you know what to do in case of fire, injury or other emergencies. Perhaps a trusted neighbour can be asked to keep an eye on you, or you could call someone close by. Figure it out *before* so that you are prepared, should any such situation arise.**

70 WHEN YOU ARE ALONE AND UNSURE...

Have you ever found yourself in a new place and suddenly felt a little shiver of fear run down your spine? Don't worry, you are not alone in feeling like that, and there's nothing wrong with you either – it is probably your sixth sense kicking in.

Look around you and learn to identify why you feel unsafe.

- Is the street too quiet?
- Are the street lights broken? Is it too dark?
- Do locals and residents around you look unfriendly, menacing or too interested in you?
- Is any stranger approaching you or trying to talk to you?
- Can you see people holding, wielding or hiding weapons?
- Do you see bottles of alcohol and/or needles strewn around?

If the answer to any of these questions is yes, you might be in danger. Trust your instincts and get out of there as fast as possible.

Remember!

- Adults never approach children for help. If any adult comes to a child 'for help', you can be sure it is an unsafe situation.
- If you feel you are being approached for money, drop a dummy wallet (with a little money in it) and run from there.
- If there are women and children around, move towards them, but leave the area as quickly as possible.
- Do not try to fight anybody who is holding a weapon. It is better to run away and escape.
- In general, avoid walking around in strange places alone. If you must explore, do wear shoes in which you can run without falling.
- Carry a mobile phone and keep family members on speed dial. Make a distress call any time you feel uneasy about your surroundings.
- Finally, if you plan to take an alternative route home from somewhere familiar, like school, do so with a friend who is older than you. Remember, taking a shortcut that makes you end up in a scary neighbourhood is not bravery or adventure, it's foolhardiness!

SafeBook Says

If you ever get lost or separated from your family in a large public place, such as a mall, an entertainment or amusement park, find your way to the Information Desk or Reception by asking. It's safer to ask people wearing a uniform that has the logo of the place.

71 WHAT TO DO IF YOU'RE BEING FOLLOWED

That hollow feeling in the pit of the stomach – the suspicion that a sinister someone is following you – is one of the worst feelings ever. But safety-smart behaviour means preparing for an emergency situation, and so, knowing what to do even under pressure.

Here's what to do:

DO

☑ Stay alert on the street. Pay attention around you. So, what do you think of walking with earphones plugged in? *Not* a good idea at all!

☑ Remember, if you feel that someone is following you, mix up your pace – hurry, then slow down, change directions. Take a pause, then turn back and look directly at the suspect. This could throw them off.

☑ **Most important:** Always head to crowded and well-lit areas, like a café or a restaurant. If the person persists in following you in, get a close look so that you can describe their appearance to the police, if needed later. Never go home directly if you think you are being followed, so that the person following you does not get to know where you stay.

☑ Remember, a better strategy is to always let your family know when you head out. Switch on your phone GPS and send your live location to close contacts.

☑ Of course, if you feel insecure at any time, pick up your phone and call the police. That's what they're there for!

DON'T

☒ Go into isolated streets. ESPECIALLY when you're in a huff or distracted.

SafeBook Says

"There are a lot of apps built for personal safety, such as Circle of 6, bSafe, Red Panic Button and others, which send your location to your trusted friends or family, or even dial the police. Scream Alarm is a handy little one-button app that emits a loud scream and wards off would-be assailants. Watch Over Me and SOS Stay Safe are apps that simply require a shake of the phone to sound an alarm and inform contacts. With Raksha, you can send out a distress signal, Smart 24x7 has a bagful of tricks, KiteString monitors inactivity and thus helps you if you panic… If you have a smartphone, use it well to keep a few safety apps handy.*"

**This list of apps is neither comprehensive nor specifically recommended, it is only indicative. There are many apps available. Please choose what suits you and your device best. – Author*

Section Ten

GENERAL

72 ELEVATOR BLUES

Elevators or lifts have been around for just over a century. They save time and energy. But an elevator is an electrical machine, so it can malfunction. Its operation can be interrupted either due to a fault in the circuit or due to a power cut. Does that mean we avoid using an elevator altogether? Errr, NO. Just be safety-smart.

So, what would you do if you got stuck in an elevator? The first, but not-so-obvious, step is to keep calm and not panic. Request co-passengers to stay calm. Most modern elevators have a backup battery so that the light and fan inside keep running even if the elevator has stopped working.

Remember!

Every elevator does have an emergency button (look for a bell symbol) to connect you to the control room via an intercom system. Press it and tell them about your location and wait. They *will*

send someone to help you out. In some cases, communication may be one-way, so you can only speak but not hear. Hence, we repeat. Do not panic. It doesn't help.

DO

- ☑ Watch your step when getting in or out of an elevator. Stand clear of the doors.
- ☑ Hold the handrails if available and move towards the back to make room for other passengers.
- ☑ Pay attention; be prepared to exit when you get to your floor.
- ☑ If the door does not open, push the 'Door Open' button. Use the button to hold the doors open for a while if you need to wait for someone else.

DON'T

- ☒ Lean on the doors.
- ☒ Use your hand or any other object to stop the door from closing.
- ☒ Push your way into a crowded elevator, wait for the next one.
- ☒ Use an elevator in case of a fire. Always take the stairs in emergency situations.

SafeBook Quiz

Do you know who invented the elevator?

73 FEVER FUNDAMENTALS

What exactly is a fever? First and foremost, it is not an illness. It is a sign of illness. It is a part of your body's defence mechanism. Body temperature rises due to chemicals released by the immune system to fight viral and bacterial infections.

Of course you will have parents and caregivers to look after you. But there are a few things you can do too. Here they are:

DO

☑ Let your parents/caregivers know. Your illness could be contagious. They may decide to give you an OTC (over-the-counter) drug like paracetamol or ibuprofen in appropriate doses to help bring your temperature down. Never exceed the recommended dosage.

☑ Drink plenty of fluids, such as water or ORS, juices, soups and so on. ORS is a solution that contains salts and sugar, and gives energy as well as hydration.

- ☑ Dip a cloth in chilled water, squeeze out the excess water and place it on the forehead and back of the neck: the body temperature actually comes down!
- ☑ Make sure you have plenty of rest, mainly bed rest. Erm…that also means staying away from all kinds of screens – phone, tabs, phablets, laptops, desktops, TV…yep – that should cover it!

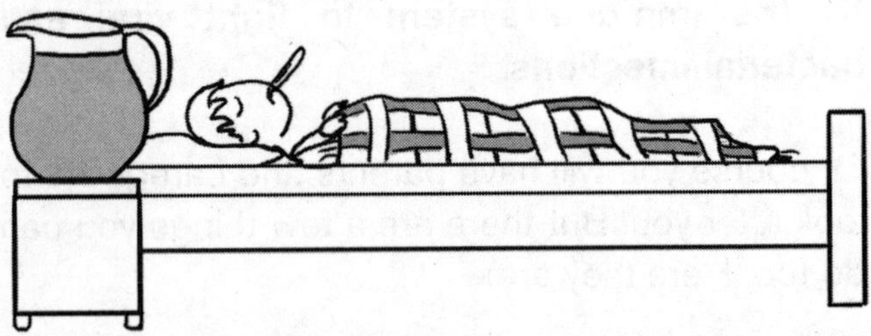

DON'T

- ☒ Have beverages like tea and coffee: they can cause further dehydration.
- ☒ Jump into cold baths or showers, unless advised by a medical practitioner. The cold, flowing water will make the blood vessels tighten and then trap body heat. The cold may also cause shivering, which can generate more heat. Odd, isn't it, but there it is!

SafeBook Says

"If the thermometer reading shows 104°F, or if the fever lasts longer than three days along with unusual, worrying symptoms such as vomiting, neck stiffness, skin rash, rapid heart rate, chills or muscle spasms, *contact your doctor immediately*. We are S-E-R-I-O-U-S."

If ORS packets are not available, you can make it at home as well. Here's the recipe from the National Health Portal of India.

Mix together *4 cupfuls (1 litre)* clean water with *six level teaspoons (1 teaspoon = 5 g)* of sugar and *½ level teaspoon of* salt. Stir until the sugar dissolves. Be very careful to mix the correct amounts. Too much sugar can worsen certain symptoms, such as diarrhoea, and too much salt can be very harmful.

74 HELP! THERE'S A CHEMICAL SPLASH ON MY SKIN!

Chemicals cause burns. If the chemical is strong or concentrated, the burn is going to be severe. Ouch! Dangerous chemicals can be found either in your school chemistry lab or even at home (drain cleaners, phenyl, paint thinners). Some chemicals can also be absorbed by the skin and lungs if you spill some chemical on yourself.

Chemicals can be very harmful and dangerous, so first of all stay away from them. Here are some more instructions to keep in mind.

DO

- ☑ Remember, cool running water helps to flush the chemical off the skin. Run it for 5 to 20 minutes depending on how bad the itch or burn is. And oh, the water needs to flow directly into a sink and not on to other body parts. Obvious.
- ☑ Remove any clothes or jewellery with chemicals on them.

☑ Cover the burn with a sterile gauze or a clean cloth. Wrap the bandage loosely, else the pressure on your skin could make it hurt worse.

☑ Contact emergency services IMMEDIATELY if the burn is deep or covers more than 3 inches, or if the chemical comes into contact with your eyes, nose or mouth.

DON'T

☒ Put an antibiotic ointment on the burn.

SafeBook Says

> **A corrosive substance is that which eats up, damages or destroys anything it touches. Corrosive chemicals can cause serious damage. If the label on any product has the symbol shown below, *do not touch it.***

Watch out for these cautionary symbols: They warn you against chemical hazards

75 TAKE A DEEEEEEEEP BREATH! OH WAIT, ARE YOU CHOKING?

What comes to your mind when you think of air pollution? Vehicle exhaust fumes? Factory smoke? Yes, sure, but here's a surprise fact: the air you breathe inside your house may be more toxic that the air outside! Is your mouth hanging open? Clamp it shut. First purify the air around you!

Indoor air pollution can be caused by lots of different things. Here's a list:

- Candle smoke
- Cleaning liquids
- Air-borne allergens (allergy-creating particles such as mould and pollen)
- Wood-burning fireplaces
- Kerosene stoves
- Fumes from what are called volatile organic compounds or VOCs – some of which are mothballs, nail polish remover, tobacco, glue, varnish and scented aerosol sprays

Inhaling these gases and chemicals for long periods could cause several ailments including severe breathing problems, runny eyes and nose, sore throat and even cancer.

Aloe vera is an air-purifying plant

DO

☑ Open windows and doors. More outdoor air coming indoors means fresher indoors. Install and run exhaust fans in kitchens and bathrooms to improve ventilation, which is a big word for circulation of air.

☑ Use air purifiers – they capture particles like dead skin, pet dander, dust and other solid things that may be floating around. They can get choked, so please do clean out their filters.

- ☑ Change the air filters of your ACs at least once a month (or once a fortnight if you live in a big city). We guarantee that your eyes will pop when you see how black and grimy they get!
- ☑ Air fresheners and scented candles give out lovely fragrances, we agree, but they also release VOCs. Use beeswax candles instead, they ionize the air – meaning, they release charged particles called ions, which help to trap dust and other yucky things in the air and reduce the toxic effect of VOCs.
- ☑ Do away with carpets if you live in a warm region – they trap pollutants, are often not cleaned and, really, why?
- ☑ Keep chemicals away from living areas. Floor cleaners, toilet cleaners, glass cleaners and bleach all contain strong chemicals that can fill your lungs with awful stuff. Keep them covered in airy spaces and use them sparingly.
- ☑ Use a dehumidifier (especially during the rainy season) to prevent the growth of mould – that's fungus, and it is very unhealthy. Pay special attention to shoes, dark spaces like the insides of cupboards, under the sink and lofts.
- ☑ We all know that plants are great, but did you know that some plants happily clean the air at home, for free, and don't even complain? Look

at the pictures below, find out about more such plants and choose the ones you want. And thank Mother Nature yet again !

A few air-purifying plants (from left): Chinese evergreen, snake plant and areca palm

SafeBook Says

"The World Health Organization has calculated that indoor air pollution kills some 4·3 million people a year in developing countries – that's a CRAZY HIGH NUMBER! It is the world's greatest environmental threat, and since women and children traditionally spend more time at home, they are the worst hit."

76 BETWEEN THE SYMBOLS: A GUIDE TO LABELS ON COSMETICS

When purchasing cosmetics, we pick brands, looks, perhaps price. But the label on the packaging contains information about their expiration date, volume, recyclability and a host of other things.

Here's an easy way to help you decipher labels.

QUICK LIST

	1. Period after opening (PAO) Symbol: Tells you how long the product stays good after opening. 'M' stands for month.		2. Also known as the Mobius loop, this symbol denotes that the product container is recyclable.
	3. Best before end of (BBE) date: The hourglass symbol followed by the date denotes the period in which the product is good from the date of manufacture.		4. Green circle and arrow: The symbol means that the manufacturer has paid a recycling organization for efficient management of their packaging waste.

5. The e-mark denotes the net quantity of a product. This symbol is found on European brands with the quantity given in terms of gram (g) or millilitres (ml).	6. The leaping bunny symbol implies that manufacturer does not test their product on animals to check for adverse reactions.
7. Fire symbol: Denotes that the product is flammable and must be kept away from flames. This is usually found on deodorants, hairspray, nail polish and their removers.	8. Ecocert is a France-based organic certification organization that certifies food products and cosmetics, among other products.
9. The 'Refer to Insert' symbol means that there is a leaflet with additional information and instruction that could not be printed on the product (usually due to lack of space).	10. The cruelty-free symbol from PETA implies that the manufacturers have not done any animal-testing of its products and also use vegan ingredients only.

SafeBook Says

> **Have you seen any other label on your cosmetic product that is not listed here? Draw it here and find out what it means.**

77 HOW TO STAY SAFE IN SCHOOL

What is the safest place to be in, apart from your home? Guess what, it's your school. Schools are built for children, and that means the materials used and spaces created are safe.

Chances are that your school has taken measures for your safety. There are no sharp edges, no breakable objects in common spaces, no dangerous liquids or gases and no unsafe details like too-slippery floors, walls or staircases without banisters or fencing from which children can fall. But there's no harm in being careful, is there?

So, while in school:

DON'T

- ☒ Run on the stairs. Instead, walk to one side, along a banister. In India, usually, stick to the banister on your left.
- ☒ Mess around with things in science labs. Chemicals in school labs are usually very mild,

but can still be dangerous if misused, if not lethal. It's no fun splashing liquids that burn a hole in your clothes – and body!

- ☒ Use stationery items to hurt each other. The compass or divider in your geometry box, sharp pencils, pen nibs and rulers can really hurt badly.
- ☒ Touch or use cleaning liquids around the school toilet. Some contain ammonia, some contain strong bleach, some contain acids, and all of them are poisonous.
- ☒ Eat while playing. This is a no-brainer. Your food can fall and be stepped on, you can gather germs in the playground that will go into your food as you eat it, and you may then fall pretty ill.
- ☒ Meddle with the electric water cooler or dispenser or go behind it for any reason. It can give you a nasty electric shock.
- ☒ Look too far down from upper floors.
- ☒ Go near the pool alone when no one is around.

The most accident-prone parts of school for all children are the playground and open areas. Remember...

DO

- ☑ Do wear shoes with neatly tied laces. Tripping over your own shoelace and falling flat on your face is very silly and very avoidable.

☑ If your school has any soft playing area like grass, sand or artificial soft turf, play there, especially if you like running around, or playing catch or other group games. Do not run on concrete. A fall there can be very painful.

DON'T

☒ Do not run around barefoot. You can get stamped on, break toenails, step on something sharp or get bitten by creepy-crawlies.

☒ Do not mess with anything made of metal, like nails, benches or gym equipment with metal sticking out, or barbed wire. If you prick your skin on metal, go to the school clinic and get a tetanus injection immediately.

☒ Do not fight or push anyone on a jungle gym or monkey bars. A fall can be very, very serious.

SafeBook Says

"The Government of India recommends that the school bag be no more than 10% of the student's body weight. Do you know your body weight? Divide it by ten. Then see if your bag weighs more or less than that!"

78 WHAT SHOULD YOU DO IF A BEE STINGS YOU?

Doesn't the very word 'sting' make you feel like going 'ouch'? There's sharp pain, as well as redness and swelling around a bee or wasp sting; this is known as a local reaction, because it's in a specific location.

Most insect stings can be treated at home with proper first aid, but some people develop an allergic reaction to the sting. Have you wondered why a bee sting hurts more than a mosquito bite? When bees sting, they release a chemical called melittin, which causes pain and a burning sensation. The

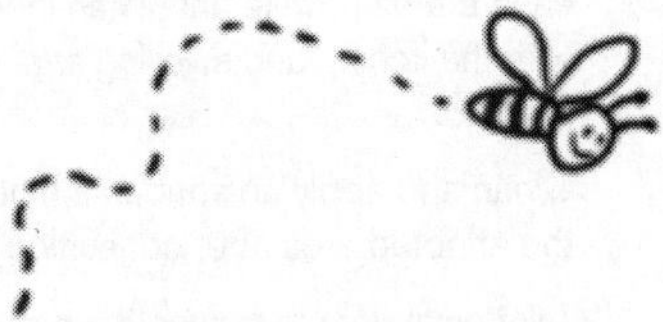

SafeBook Says

"Do you know that it is actually possible to avoid being stung, or at least reduce your chances? The solution is almost ridiculously simple: do not wear bright colours or scented perfumes in areas that have a lot of bees."

longer the stinger stays in the skin, the more toxin it releases.

Quick Tips

In all these cases, do get an adult to help.

Kind of reaction and what to do	If you do not have an allergic reaction to the sting:	If you do have an allergic reaction to the sting:
Ask a grown-up to gently scrape the stinger off with a dull-edged object like a credit card. If it's not removed, the stinger will continue to release toxins and cause pain.	Yes	Yes
Apply a cold compress/ice on the area to ease the pain. Take antihistamines to help with the itching and swelling *after consulting a doctor.*	Yes	Yes
Clean and apply an antibiotic ointment on the affected area after consulting a doctor.	Yes	Yes
Take painkillers to reduce the pain.	If needed, and on doctor's advice	Yes
Wash the sting site with soap and water. If you haven't received a tetanus shot in the last ten years, get a shot within a couple of days.	Yes	Yes
Get a tetanus shot.	Not required	If you haven't had one in 10 years, take a shot within a couple of days.

79 HOW TO BE SAFE AROUND A STRANGE DOG

Dogs are known and loved for their loyalty and fondness for human company. The number of people who have a dog as a pet has gone up in recent years, thanks to greater access to information, and there are now nearly 20 million dog owners in India.

So… is there a flip side? Unfortunately, yes. Dogs do bite sometimes, and the bite carries the risk of rabies and other viral and bacterial infections such as norovirus and salmonella.

Apart from pet dogs that live in homes, there are street dogs and lost pets. How do we know which is which?

- Street dogs live, well, on the streets. They rely on the generosity of the people around them to feed them, and they are usually not vaccinated against rabies.
- Lost or abandoned pets could have a collar around their neck, look cleaner and have the appearance of pedigree.

Here's a small list of dos and don'ts when you are approached by a strange dog:

DO

- ☑ Keep calm. Dogs can sense fear and could get agitated by your fear.
- ☑ Look out for behavioural signs to assess the dog's attitude. Assess a dog's body language. Aggressive dogs can be like this:

Head low, teeth bared, growling

Snarling, barking

- ☑ A dog that comes wagging its tail and seems playful is likely to do you no harm.
- ☑ If a dog approaches you, stand still and calm, let it sniff if it wants to. Slowly walk away from the dog, without making any sudden movements or eye contact or noise.
- ☑ If you happen to walk on a road where there are lots of barking or growling dogs, cross over to the other side. Dogs are more confident when in a pack and even timid dogs could become belligerent. If you are very afraid, take help from people nearby.

DON'T

- ☒ Make any hand gestures that may frighten the dog, such as flapping, shooing, raising an arm menacingly or waving your fist or a stick in its face.
- ☒ Yell at the dog. Speak in a soothing and reassuring manner.
- ☒ Bother a dog when it's eating or go near its food. Dogs are extremely protective about their food and can turn aggressive if someone interferes with their food.
- ☒ Disturb a dog while it's sleeping.
- ☒ Go near a mother dog when she is with her pups. Animal mothers are very protective and anyone approaching their babies is considered a threat.
- ☒ Hit the dog. Use objects such as a bag to fend off an attack by a dog. If you aren't carrying any object, use your forearm to protect your face and neck.
- ☒ Ever run if a dog starts running towards you, it will only provoke the dog to chase you.

SafeBook Says

"Avoid going near an injured dog if you lack experience. If you see a dog in distress, you can contact the local NGOs working towards animal rescue such as PETA India and Blue Cross of India, among others. Seek help from others to take the dog to a vet and get it treated."

80 HOW TO TAKE CARE AGAINST COVID-19

A common parting phrase used to be, 'Take care!'. That is, until 2020. To that was added another two-word phrase, 'Stay safe'. COVID-19 has forced us to focus on safety the way no war, disease or disaster has ever done.

What is COVID-19?

COVID-19 is an acronym for COronaVIrus Disease 2019, because the first cases identified date back to 2019. Declared as a pandemic by the World Health Organization in March 2020, the novel Coronavirus disease (COVID-19) is an infectious lung-affecting disease caused by the SARS Coronavirus.

With worldwide onset of COVID-19, the world quickly learned a new vocabulary: 'coronavirus', 'lockdown', 'pandemic', 'social distancing' and the names of a host of medicines, medical equipment and procedures. Even as vaccination has helped the number of cases to reduce worldwide, the

World Health Organization (WHO) has said that COVID-19 is here to stay.

How does one get COVID-19? When an infected person coughs, sneezes or exhales, the tiny droplets generated in the process spread the infection. So your chances of getting infected are high when you are very near them. You can also get infected if you touch your eyes, nose or mouth after touching a (very) recently contaminated surface.

While COVID-19 affects different people differently, the most common symptoms include fever, headache, cough, difficulty in breathing, and loss of smell and taste, which develop in a period of 2-14 days after getting infected. A majority of people only experience mild to moderate symptoms and recover without hospitalization. Older people and/or those with underlying medical problems are more likely to develop serious illness.

The best way to prevent the spread of the virus is to maintain personal hygiene and get vaccinated as soon as possible.

DO

☑ Wash your hands as often as possible with soap, even if they look clean. If there's no soap, use an alcohol-based hand rub or sanitizer (with at least 60% alcohol).

☑ Wear a mask in public spaces. Always. We cannot stress this enough. The mask must cover your nose, mouth and chin properly. Clean your hands before you put the mask on, and before and after you take it off.

☑ Stay at least one metre away from others.

☑ Cover your mouth with a handkerchief/tissue while coughing or sneezing, or, if you don't have one, with your bent elbow. Throw used tissues into a closed bin immediately after use.

Wear a mask, sanitize your hands regularly and sneeze into your elbow

☑ Consult a doctor if you have fever, cough or are unable to breathe comfortably. Isolate yourself from the rest of your family members – that is, move to a separate room and ideally use a separate bathroom. Get an RT-PCR test done to check if you are COVID-positive.

☑ Use a disinfectant to clean surfaces such as door handles, taps and phones – these are touched frequently.

☑ Finally, do go to the nearest vaccination centre and get your jab as soon as you are eligible. All vaccines have been declared safe and effective by medical authorities, and they are our biggest weapon against COVID.

DON'T

- ☒ Keep touching your eyes, nose and mouth.
- ☒ Use masks with valves.*
- ☒ Visit crowded and closed places. It's always better to meet people outside.
- ☒ Organize social gatherings at home if possible.
- ☒ Spit in public places. Let us rephrase. Don't spit in public spaces ever. That's just *eww*.
- ☒ Shake hands or hug people when you greet them. Our namasté is a wonderful thing!
- ☒ Meet people who have fever or a cough. Instead, do give them a copy of *The SafeBook* for easy reference!

SafeBook Says

"If you need information about COVID-19, you can contact the 24 X 7 COVID helpline of the Government of India: 1075 (toll-free) or +91-11-23978046."

After the deadly Delta variant, a new, highly infectious variant of the coronavirus, labelled Omicron, has been detected. Scientists and WHO experts agree that COVID is not going away anytime soon, but it is likely to become endemic. Be that as it may, stay safe, and we mean it!

See the next chapter: 'Why You Should Mask Up'

81 WHY YOU SHOULD MASK UP

The biggest visible difference since COVID-19 has been the appearance of masks to cover the lower parts of faces. Until we truly see the back of the pandemic, masks are here to stay.

With the variety of masks available in the market, how to choose the most suitable ones to ensure our safety?

Quick Checklist

- Choose a mask that is correct for your face size. Your nose and mouth should be covered, and your head/ears should not hurt.
- Your mask should have two or more layers of breathable fabric, and you should be able to breathe through the mask. So do not buy masks made of vinyl, plastic or other materials that prevent you from breathing.
- If you wear glasses, the mask could have a nose wire that would help the mask fit snugly as well so it does not cause the glasses to mist up.

- Do not wear a mask with valves or vents that allow air to be exhaled. They defeat the very purpose of a COVID-mask.

Now that we have sorted *which* mask to wear, it is important to understand *how* to wear the mask.

Quick Tips

– Wear it so that it covers your nose *and* mouth.

So **do not** wear it:

– Under the nose
– Only on your nose
– On your chin
– Dangling from one ear
– On your forehead
– Around your neck
– Over the arm

SafeBook Says

"If you feel your mask does not protect you adequately, you can wear a surgical use-and-throw mask with a cloth one *over* it."

Type of Masks

Scarf & Fabric Mask

PROS: Washable, comfortable, blocks coarse droplets
CONS: Doesn't block fine and ultrafine droplets

Surgical Mask

PROS: Two protective layers, blocks coarse and fine droplets
CONS: Only one use, doesn't block ultrafine droplets

N95 and Similar

PROS: Many protective layers, seals tight, blocks coarse, fine and ultrafine droplets
CONS: Must seal tight, one use, costs more

ANSWERS

FIRE

Page 16: 1. F 2. T 3. T 4. T 5. F

Page 18: *Did you say Flour?*

Oops. It can explode and cause the fire to *spread*!

Did you say Baking Soda?

You are a star! Yes, it may be used to put out a SMALL kitchen grease fire because it releases carbon dioxide, smothers the fire by cutting off oxygen and makes the flames die down. Remember that **baking *soda*** and **baking *powder*** are two different things.

Page 31: Wood, paper, cotton, oil

Page 40: 1E, 2D, 3A, 4B, 5C

HOME

Page 50: Low

Page 55: Mercury

ELECTRICITY

Page 72: Silver. Copper is most commonly used to make wires because (a) there is more copper than silver found on Earth, which makes silver much more expensive, (b) silver, when exposed to air, tarnishes, and eventually degrades, much faster than copper, and (c) copper is only very slightly less conductive than silver, so it is a great option. Silver is used for short, highly specialized and sensitive electrical systems, like in some automobile contact systems.

Page 80: C

Page 85: B. In distilled water, there are no impurities, there are no ions (atoms or molecules with an electric charge). There are only neutral (no charge) water molecules and these neutral molecules don't have charge, so distilled water does not conduct electricity.

Page 88: Electricity on power lines needs to reach the ground to complete the circuit. Birds sit on the same line, not across two lines, and their claws do not touch the ground, so although there is current flowing through the line, it does not give a shock to the birds. As a human, sorry, dear friend, you are too heavy to sit on a line and *not* complete the circuit!

Page 93: Carbon monoxide

Page xxx: Alessandro Volta, an Italian physicist and chemist, and a pioneer of electricity and power.

ROAD

Page 104: P, P, A, P, P, A

Page 108: Vehicle B will exert less pressure, because the tyres exert pressure over a greater surface area.

Page 120: (c)

THE INTERNET

Page 148: DO: 3, 5, 6; DON'T: 1, 2, 4

NATURAL DISASTER

Page 179: Richter Scale, developed by Charles Francis Richter in 1935. It calculates the magnitude, or size and strength. But that is a slightly dated, and inadequate, scale. There are other, more precise scales, like the moment magnitude scale (MMS) and the Mercalli Scale, which measure the intensity of an earthquake.

Perhaps most interesting is the (Enhanced) Rohn Emergency Scale, which quantifies the magnitude or intensity of any emergency, including earthquakes, and proposes a mathematical model that accounts for accurate forecasting, monitors the development of the emergency, and the planning and execution of the handling of measures to respond to the emergency.

GENERAL

Page 214: Elisha Graves Otis. After working in a gristmill, a sawmill, as a dollmaker and as a maker of bedsteads, he and his sons made a safety elevator (initially for things, not people) that would not go into free-fall if the hoisting cable snapped. In 1853, he demonstrated his invention in New York, at the World's Fair, by standing in an elevator and then ordering that the cable be cut, in front of an amazed crowd!

KEYWORD SEARCH